Robert Gilmour LeTourneau, 7,000 feet up.

Foreword

By H. A. IRONSIDE, LITT.D.

Pastor, Moody Memorial Church, Chicago

IT WAS in the city of Duluth, about the close of the last century, that I first became acquainted with the LeTourneau family. I was in that city ministering the Word of God to a small assembly of believers with which Mr. and Mrs. LeTourneau were connected. I vaguely recall the subject of the present biography, Robert G. LeTourneau, as a restless, energetic youngster, stockily built, who did not have much desire to come into intimate contact with the visiting preacher. Some years afterwards I became better acquainted with him, when the family had moved to Portland, Oregon, and then later to California.

As I look back over the years, I marvel at the wonderful way in which God has displayed His grace in this man. I am reminded of what George Muller said in regard to his orphanage work in Bristol, England. He declared that the outstanding reason which led him to decide to count on God to supply all financial need in answer to prayer, apart from any personal solicitation, was in order that he might demonstrate to a gainsaying, unbelieving generation that God is still the Living God. It seems to me that in a somewhat different way this is what we see manifested in

3

the life of R. G. LeTourneau. What thoughtful person can doubt, upon becoming familiar with the striking facts recorded in this volume, that a living, loving, all-powerful, personal God has been watching over this man from childhood up to the present moment. It was His grace that convicted the boy of sin and led him to trust the Saviour. It was the same grace that restored his soul when he had drifted into a careless, easy-going Christian profession, in which he had no real testimony for the Lord.

When at last awakened by the Spirit of God and led to acknowledge the Lordship of Christ over his life, what marvelous evidences have been given throughout the years, proving that there is indeed a God who answers prayer and who never goes back upon His word. He has declared, "Them that honor me, I will honor, and they that despise me shall be lightly esteemed." In large measure, the subject of this biography has endeavored to honor God, and He, in turn, has honored His devoted servant, giving him seemingly almost unlimited powers of endurance and using him in a manner which none could have foreseen in his early days.

LeTourneau has never aimed at becoming personally wealthy; yet God has entrusted him with millions of money, which he has sought to use conscientiously for His glory. His life story should be an encouragement to Christian young people everywhere, impressing upon heart and mind the truth of the Saviour's words, "Seek ye first the kingdom of God and His righteousness, and all these things shall be added unto you." In other words, Christianity is not simply a spiritual fire insurance policy, whereby one may hope to escape judgment and find salvation in a future world, but it is a livable experience suited to all the exigencies of life here on earth. This business man and mechanical genius has demonstrated the reality of spiritual things in a real workaday world. Personally, my own life has been enriched by knowing him through the years, and I am thankful to have the privilege of commending, in this way, his testimony as embodied in this book. It shows what God can do with a life that is wholly yielded to His control. This is not to say that Mr. LeTourneau has always understood the will of God and obeyed it in every particular. He would be the last man to pretend to anything of the sort. As I have known him through the years, he has always been ready to acknowledge frankly his own failures and shortcomings. But it is one thing for a man to fail at times in apprehending the will of God and quite another to be living in self-will. The whole trend of this man's life, since he yielded himself to the Lord, has been that of consecration to the will of God. If at times he has fallen, he has fallen face forward and risen again to press more steadily on his way, as one who could say with a saint of old, "Rejoice not over me, O mine enemy, for if I fall I shall rise again." And as with purpose of heart he has pressed along the upward way, God has delighted to show

Himself strong in behalf of one who has trusted Him so fully.

In this he may well be an example to us all. It would not be irreverent for him to say to others with the apostle Paul, "Follow me as I follow Christ." Thus pursuing the path of dependence on the Living God, one will know for himself the truth of the words, "The path of the just is as the shining light, which shineth brighter and brighter unto the perfect day." If any be encouraged by this record to seek to emulate the faith and devotion of its subject, I am sure that he who has consented somewhat unwillingly to the publication of his life story will feel more than repaid.

Contents

1st Note Page 126

auto
accide—
PG. 80

See 175

181

7

Acknowledgment

THE author is indebted to many friends and business associates of Mr. LeTourneau for invaluable assistance in supplying material for the present volume.

Space does not permit listing the names of all those who cheerfully gave of their time and effort. However, credit must be given to Dr. Harold Strathearn for making the original suggestion to compile this history.

A. W. L.

Boston, Mass.

List of Illustrations

FACING
PAGE

Consecration

THERE is an old Dutch picture of a little child dropping a cherished toy from his hands; and, at first sight, his action seems unintelligible, until, at the corner of the picture, the eye is attracted to a white dove winging its flight toward the emptied outstretched hands. Similarly, we are prepared to forego a good deal when once we catch sight of the spiritual acquisitions which beckon to us. And this is the true way to reach consecration and surrender. Do not ever dwell on the *giving up* side, but on the *receiving* side. Keep in mind the meaning of the old Hebrew word for consecration, *to fill the hands*. There will not be much trouble in getting men to empty their hands of wood, hay, stubble, if they see that there is a chance of filling them with the treasures which gleam from the faces or lives of others, or which call to them from the pages of Scripture. The world pities us because it sees only what we give up; but it would withhold its sympathy if it could also see how much we receive—"good measure, pressed down, and running over, given into our bosoms."

F. B. Meyer.

I

Dirt in the Carbureter

TWO MEN, father and son, sat talking one Saturday evening in the library of their home in the city of Boston.

"What do you know about the man who is to speak at tomorrow night's service?" asked one of them.

"Nothing," answered the elder, "except what the pastor said about him. He told us the man is the active head of a big manufacturing company who has been enormously successful in business and that he attributes his success to the fact that he made God his business partner. He also said he makes week-end trips to churches all over the country in his own airplane, at his own expense, to present his personal testimony as a Christian."

The young man smiled.

"I wanted to see if you knew as much as I know about him. One of my Tech profs knows him personally. He told me he designs and builds road machinery which literally moves mountains. A man, with one of these machines, can move 100,000 pounds of dirt at a speed of 25 miles an hour. The prof said that this man started with nothing, is now wealthy, and contributes 90 per cent of what he makes to Christian work. He has three big plants, employs thousands of workmen, and yet is able to run his business without labor trouble. I'd like to hear him and learn more about him. He must have something."

"Well! Let us, you and I, go and hear him then."

They did. The church was filled. The pastor introduced the speaker. He was big and husky, about middle age, and everything about him looked strong and well put together. Evidently an outdoor man, used to using his hands. He moved as though he expected things to get out of his way. He wasted no time in introductory remarks. He had traveled thousands of miles by air, he said, to deliver a spiritual message. He came directly to the point of what he had to say:

"When I was a young fellow about twenty years old," he said, "I decided I wanted to be an automobile mechanic and got a job in a garage. One evening, when I was on duty all alone, a man called up and said: 'My car is broken down. Send a mechanic to fix it.' I answered, 'I haven't anyone to send. I'm the only one here.' He said, 'Don't leave me stranded here this way; give me some sort of help.' I replied, 'All right. I'll lock up and be over.'

"At that time I hadn't learned much about a car. I didn't know where to look for the magneto or the carbureter. Fearing this man might expect too much

UPPER. Robert's father and mother, Mr. and Mrs. Caleb LeTourneau.
LOWER. Robert's brothers and sisters (Robert, center of top row).

UPPER. Stockton garage, where young LeTourneau started as automobile mechanic.
CENTER. The old Moss Avenue Shop, Stockton.
LOWER. Shop built at Roosevelt Street and Wilson Way, Stockton.

of me, I explained, when I found him, that I was not a full-fledged mechanic. That was a great mistake. Never apologize for what you don't know. I never made that mistake again. He said, 'Don't touch that motor then!' He went to work on it himself. He cranked and he fussed until he wore himself out. He threw the crank down on the pavement and said, 'Go ahead and see what you can do with it.'

"It was one of those old-time Cadillacs and while he'd been fussing I studied that engine. I saw where the magneto was located, and the carbureter, and where all the wires went. So when he gave me the signal, I was ready to go. I said to myself, *I don't know too much about this machine, but I have sense enough to take it apart and clean it up and put it together again.*

"I started in. I took the carbureter apart, cleaned everything very carefully, and laid the pieces side by side. Inside the carbureter I found a tiny speck of dirt. I took it out and put everything back just as I found it. Every screw back where it belonged. I replaced the carbureter. Then I took the crank and turned the motor over and away it went, as pretty as you please.

"That man was so happy over the way I'd fixed his engine that whenever he got in trouble with his car after that, he'd call up and say, 'Send me that kid.'

"Friends, listen to me: I want you to get the meaning of the story I've just told you. I could not do a thing for that man until he was willing to let me help him. I might have had all the skill in the world. As long as he said, 'Don't touch it!' I couldn't help him. My skill could be of no use to him until he was willing to say, 'Go ahead!'

"That's the way it is with our lives. God Himself can't help us until we are ready to let Him. Why? Because God has given us the power of choice. He gave us that prerogative and it is up to us. God won't force us. You can accept or refuse His offer, just as you choose.

"I trust that there are some here tonight who are thinking it over seriously and are ready to let God help them. Folks, I hope you get the lesson out of this story. That speck of dirt in the carbureter was the cause of the trouble that man was having with his engine—that tiny speck was able to stop that big machine.

"My business is manufacturing road-building machinery. We employ Diesel engines in some of these machines. In a Diesel engine there is a tiny hole, about $6/1000$ of an inch in diameter, through which the fuel has to pass. A little speck of dirt no bigger than $6/1000$ of an inch is all it takes to stop one of those powerful engines. I say to you it doesn't take much to cut off the power between a human being and God. It may be a small thing—ever so small— and yet it will stop the power.

"When God talks to us about some little thing in our lives, that's the time we must give it up. Paltry things must be given up if we are to enjoy a close fellowship with God. I am not here to say that I have done everything God has told me to do, but I am still trying. I am asking Him to show me day by day what He wants me to do. This is the only way to live."

At the close of the service, father and son joined with a large part of the audience in waiting their turn to meet the speaker. He seemed willing to talk with everyone present.

On their way home the younger man asked:

"What did you think of him?"

"That story he told shows he is a good mechaanic," replied the father. "I was especially interested in the application he made from it in portraying the Creator as the great Master Mechanic, Who, when we, the creatures He has fashioned, break some moral law, or commit some sinful act, is not satisfied merely with helping us to overcome that special fault, but goes to the source of our wrongdoing, and changes our sinful hearts.

"I would like to know more about him and something about his early life. A noted clergyman once said that if one would become great, he must choose the right parents. I can imagine that a boy with the energy and initiative that this boy possessed must have kept his parents wondering what he would do next."

Because many people have felt as this father felt and have expressed themselves as wanting to know more about the background and activities of the man who thrilled that Boston congregation that night, this book has come into being.

The boy, they say, is father to the man. When we look at a man and wonder, "How did he get like that?" the answer in many cases is, "He got like that when he was a boy!"

UPPER. First LeTourneau Scraper, the Gondola, 1922.
LOWER. First LeTourneau self-propelled Scraper, forerunner of
    Tournapull, 1923.

UPPER. First cable-operated Scraper, 1928-29.
LOWER. First tractor-drawn Scraper with pneumatic tires, 1932.

II

The Twig is Bent

THE SPEAKER before the Boston congregation whose address was reported in part in the preceding chapter was Robert Gilmour LeTourneau. Last year he preached over five hundred times in widely separated parts of the country, at the same time giving his personal attention to the management of his manufacturing enterprises in California, Illinois and Georgia. In order to make time for the demands of his business and the carrying out of his evangelistic activities, he uses his own airplane, pays his own expenses, and carries with him his own singers. He tells his story before all kinds of gatherings and denominational groups from Portland, Maine, to San Francisco, from Sault Saint Marie to the Rio Grande. Besides this, he holds gospel meetings in his own factories and gives his Christian testimony to his own employees.

"As the twig is bent the tree's inclined," said Pope; and Solomon, inspired by the Holy Spirit said: "Train up a child in the way he should go: and when he is old, he will not depart from it" (Proverbs 22:6).

What of this early training in the case of R. G. Le-
Tourneau?

He had the great advantage of being born of
Christian parents. His grandfather and grandmother
on his father's side were members of cultured Hugue-
not families in France. They came to Canada and
settled in Quebec, where the grandfather served for a
time as teacher in the Grand Ligne Mission, a Prot-
estant institution. Here he also preached. Ill health,
however, made it necessary for the family to move to
Richford, Vermont, where for a time the grandfather
maintained a boarding school. Increasing illness at
length incapacitated the grandfather for teaching, the
boarding school had to be given up, and a farm was
taken. This farm later became the home of one of
the sons of the grandparents, Caleb, father of Robert,
and on this farm, November 30, 1888, R. G. Le-
Tourneau was born.

On his mother's side, Mr. LeTourneau descended
from people of similar Christian character. The
grandfather, a farmer, was as well a keen Scotch
theologian who had a reputation among his friends
and neighbors as "The Bible Concordance" because
of his familiarity with the Scriptures and his ability
to quote chapter and verse. The grandmother was
distinguished for an unusual zeal in Christian work,
her church being her supreme interest throughout a
long life.

From his father, Mr. LeTourneau inherited his
aggressive disposition and his aptitude for mechanics.

From his mother came his dynamic enthusiasm and buoyant optimism.

R. G. LeTourneau was number four in a family of eight children, five sons and three daughters. There was never a dull moment in the LeTourneau household. Five robust and energetic sons, to say nothing of the girls, provided plenty of excitement, often taxing the mother's resourcefulness to maintain discipline. It was her responsibility to act in the dual capacity of high priestess and police officer in the father's absence, a particularly trying period occurring when the father made an extensive western trip to seek a more favorable locality for his home. He was gone for a long period, during which the mother, no matter how driven by her multitudinous household tasks, carried on as head of her spiritual house and kept the fires of worship burning on the family altar. As a result of the father's investigations, the family moved from Richford to Duluth, Minnesota, and here Robert spent his boyhood until he was fifteen, when the family moved again, this time to Portland, Oregon.

Several incidents occurred during these early years, which, if briefly referred to in passing, will, it is hoped, throw fuller light on the character of the man that was to be.

One of these incidents goes back almost to babyhood. Robert was not quite two years old, and sick enough with one of those maladies of early childhood to warrant the calling in of the family doctor. After the doctor's departure, the mother, in attempting to carry out his directions and administer the medicine he left, found that her baby had his own ideas and showed unmistakable signs of desiring to stick to them, doctor's orders or no doctor's orders. A battle royal between mother and child resulted, after an all-night siege, in compromise. Robert's prolonged resistance to his mother's efforts to get him to take his medicine reduced him to such a state of weakness that his mother became alarmed and prayed he might regain strength enough to renew the battle. He did. This early evidence of will power was the forerunner of that indomitable perseverance which now characterizes many of his actions in mature life.

Inquisitiveness is another LeTourneau trait which manifested its existence during these early years. His insatiable curiosity tried his mother's patience in her own home and caused her much embarrassment when visiting in the homes of other members of the family. A great-aunt told her, "You certainly have the makings of a great explorer in that child. Some day he may become another Livingstone." An uncle, engaged in building a new barn and annoyed by Robert's climbing around on the upper beams, said to his mother, "If that boy isn't kept away from here, he'll have a broken neck." Trying to find out what things were made of was a passion with him in childhood and has no doubt been of great value to him in his mechanical career. Another uncle became a victim of Robert's curiosity to test the strength of glass against the impact of stones. This uncle raised vegetables for market and the sight of his glass-covered hotbeds was a temptation not to be resisted by boyish flesh and blood until he had broken every pane. Some years later, this uncle received a generous check during a time of sickness in the uncle's family which compensated a thousand times over for the damage done by that youthful prank.

Restlessness seems to have been more pronounced in Robert's case than in other boys. A friend of the family, amused at his irrepressible energy, exclaimed: "Robert, if you will sit down in that chair and keep still for five minutes, I'll give you five cents." At the end of five minutes Robert observed: "I'll sit still for five minutes more for another nickel." At meal time, with the meal consumed, he would sit at the table stamping his feet on the floor and saying over and over, "What can I *do*, Mama? What can I *do*?" The desire to be always occupied taxed his mother's ingenuity to the limit. Another of Robert's victims was a heifer called "Pete," belonging to the family, which he loved to ride bare back. Pete turned out to be something of a bucking broncho, however. One day he harnessed her to a snowplow, thinking he'd open up the roads. She tacked and bucked, careened off the road, zig-zagged across the fields, broke the rope of the plow, and, leaving the driver stranded, raced back to her stall.

Robert's father, realizing that a boy of his energy and restlessness must have an outlet, worked out a program of daily chores. But tasks like sawing wood held little attraction for him and only touched his interest when a fishing trip lay in prospect at the conclusion of the task. Another uncle recites the unexpected effect of imposing an irksome task on a boy of Robert's imaginative temperament. Robert and one of his brothers took turns in carrying water for the family supply from a near-by mineral spring. One day when it was the brother's turn to carry the water, Robert's father, not realizing it was the brother's turn, asked Robert to do it. When he protested, the father suggested that it might not do him any harm to take his brother's place for once. Robert thought this an imposition. So he got a neighbor's boy to help him, and between them, after arduous efforts, they pumped the spring empty. Then Robert went home and reported the spring empty. His mother, incredulous, made a visit of inspection and was obliged to confirm Robert's word. The mystery, in the absence of drought or earthquake, remained a mystery until the next day, when, it being the brother's turn to carry water, the spring was found to be full again. What the consequences to Robert were, or whether the deception was ever discovered, has not been revealed. The point of the story is that Robert did not want to tell a lie. And didn't. The spring was empty, as he claimed.

Complete absorption in the task at hand is another of the LeTourneau characteristics which gave evidence of its existence during early years. Even at play, he played as though his life depended upon the issue. A boy for whose intelligence he had not a high regard beat him at checkers. He resolved that such a thing must never happen again and became so obsessed with the determination to win that he could not sleep and lay awake all night making imaginary moves. On another occasion, while swimming in Lake Superior, he determined to learn how to dive, and dived into the water with such force and recklessness that he hit a rock and nearly scalped himself. He climbed out, reached home without help, and when his condition was discovered, a surgeon was called and took thirteen stitches in his scalp. The scar remains to this day.

One time, at the age of thirteen, he ran away from home. He had some arguments with his father and got an idea into his head that his father didn't care for him any more, and he decided to leave. He found a farm a few miles away where he could work for his room and board, and went there and began making his own way. Evidently his parents weren't very much worried, for Robert was permitted to stay. He hadn't been away very long when Thanksgiving Day arrived. It was a LeTourneau custom to hold a family reunion on this day, when all the cousins and the uncles and the aunts, with their children, came together for a big Thanksgiving dinner. Robert got to thinking how embarrassed his father and mother would feel to have the family all present and Robert not there. So he decided to return home just for the day. He did that, enjoyed himself as though nothing were wrong, and when the day was over, began thinking about going back to the farm. The Thanksgiving reunion had been held at the home of a relative, not his own home, and in order to reach the farm he had to pass his home. He walked along with his own family until they reached their house, when his father said, "You'd better come in and spend the night, Bob, and then go on in the morning." It was a cold Minnesota night, walking on alone didn't seem so attractive, he had liked being back for the day; so he decided to go in. After he was in, he realized his father did care for him, and that he had been a lot better off at home than away from home, and that maybe he'd better stay.

Robert left school at fourteen, while in the eighth grade. When he was fifteen the family moved to Portland, Oregon. Sitting in school palled on him. He was full of physical energy and wanted to be doing something. He decided he would be an iron molder. Quitting school abruptly, he went to work in a foundry to serve a four-year apprenticeship. Here he found an outlet for his superfluous energy. The heavy physical work of the foundry exactly suited his lively and restless nature. He preferred twelve hours a day at muscular activity to book study. He had served about half of his time as an apprentice when he had the experience which changed the whole course of his life. This young man, strong of body, powerful of will, impatient of restraint, ambitious and

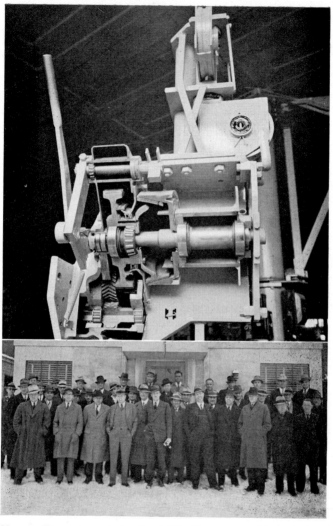

Upper. The main control unit of all LeTourneau machines, designed in a few minutes as the result of inspiration obtained at a meeting of the Stockton mission.

Lower. Sales meeting at Peoria, addressed by R. G. LeTourneau on value of unit in competition.

UPPER. First Peoria plant, erected in 1935.
LOWER. Dedication services in third addition to Peoria plant, March 1940, ex-President Herbert Hoover speaking to audience of 6,000 people.

rebellious, obstinate and courageous, imaginative and talented beyond his years, came suddenly to the Valley of Decision.

He said of himself at this time: "I was raised in a Christian home by a father and mother who loved Jesus and served Him with all their hearts. We had a family altar where we worshiped God. Father prayed and asked God to make his children useful in His kingdom. In spite of that, at the age of sixteen I found myself on the wrong road going the wrong way. I knew the right way but I'd forget about it."

The story of what happened to him at this time is best told in his own words:

"About the time I was sixteen, I began to realize that something was wrong in my life. I tried to turn over a new leaf many times, but each time I failed and each time I got worse. It wasn't that I didn't know the Bible or the way of salvation. The trouble was I knew it too well. In our home we had had to memorize Scripture and I had memorized a great deal of Scripture. But I recited it in a parrot-like way. I knew the words but they had no meaning for me. Revival meetings would come to town and I would go and get all worked up; but after the revival I'd go back to my old kind of life.

"Then a special revival came and everybody said, 'Are you going tonight?' and I said, 'Oh, yes, I guess so.' I went for four nights and then decided I wasn't getting anywhere. I was looking for something but I didn't know exactly what. I thought I was seeking after God but I was really seeking after the things which He had. The next night I stayed home and thought the whole thing over. I saw myself going down into sin and realized I was a lost sinner. The next night I went to the meeting and when the altar call was made, I went forward. The workers asked me, 'Do you believe that Christ died for sinners?' But I knew all the Scripture answers. There was something between my soul and salvation. I couldn't seem to get it; it wasn't *real* to me. I went home from that meeting that night and went to bed and as I lay there, this thought came to me: 'If I should die tonight, I would go out into a lost eternity. Hell would be worse for me than for anyone else because I had heard the Gospel and rejected it.'

"Then I cried out in desperation to God, 'Lord, save me or I perish.' Right there something happened. The glory of the Lord broke over me and the full reality of salvation came into my soul. My first thought was of my mother, who had been praying for my salvation for a long time. I thought she might be praying for me at that moment. I got out of bed and ran to her bedroom. 'Mother,' I said, 'it's all settled now. You don't need to pray for me any more. I am saved and on my way to heaven.'

"How glad I am that we have a Know-So salvation and that we don't have to *wish* we are saved or *wonder* if we are saved. But we can say with Paul, 'I know whom I have believed, and am persuaded that he is able to keep that which I have committed unto him

against that day.' Before I was saved I was churched
and bibleized, but I had never *experienced* salvation.
Since that night I have never doubted that my sins
were washed away."

His mother wept tears of joy. This was the answer
to her prayers. "The lion," she said, "is changed into
a lamb." To see this self-confident youth, accus-
tomed to conquering everything in his path, now con-
quered by the love of Christ, was indeed a miracle of
grace to those who beheld it. Rebellion gave place to
a yielding spirit. The selfish cry of his youth, "What
can *I* do?" was replaced by the cry of the Apostle Paul
on the Damascus road, "Lord, what wilt *thou* have
me to do?"

Shortly after Robert's conversion at sixteen, the
foundry in which he was working at the time was
burned. He had two years to serve to complete his
apprenticeship. He tried other foundries in Portland but could find nothing. He thought of going
to San Francisco and finding work there. When he
mentioned it to his father and mother, they were
none too pleased at the prospect of having him go so
far away, but at length consented. He said of this cir-
cumstance, "I was sure they would have put up a
fight if I had asked to go a few months before, but
now that I was saved, they knew I had something to
help me and keep me straight." He found work in
San Francisco and after two more years of apprenticeship, he won his card as a master molder. He was
in the city during the earthquake and fire and tells a

graphic story of how the Lord saved his life in that experience.

He awoke from sleep one night to find the house in which he lived sinking into the ground. He was in the second story and by the time the house had sunk to that level, he gathered together what he could of his personal belongings, stepped out of his window on to the sidewalk, and traveled seven miles through falling debris and past burning buildings till he came to safety. He felt that his life had been saved by divine intervention. The earthquake occurred on April 18, 1906, and the resulting fire destroyed $400,000,000 of property and many lives.

With his apprenticeship finished, Robert wondered what he could do next. He was a competent master molder, thoroughly familiar with pattern making, foundry procedures and the physical properties of castings. Subjects like metallurgy and mechanics excited his imagination. He had developed a keen interest in making things while employed in the foundry, and during this time he had made the patterns, molds and castings, and taking them to a nearby machine shop, had machined and assembled them into a small steam engine.

Casting about for something to do, he spent about a year on a farm in the San Joaquin Valley, near Stockton, California. The desirability of having a better education was borne in upon him at this time, and he got hold of a correspondence course and began to study. He was working on a contract to cut up one

Upper. R. G. LeTourneau and ex-President Herbert Hoover.
Lower. Dr. Harold Strathearn and R. G. receiving tribute of flowers.

Upper. Evelyn Peterson (second from right at top), her father and
mother, brothers and sister. Top row, left, Ray Peterson, Vice-
President of R. G. LeTourneau, Inc. (Recently resigned.)

Lower. Left, Evelyn at 15, on graduation from public school; right,
at 18, with oldest son, Caleb, age three months, who died shortly
thereafter.

hundred cords of wood. He would work at splitting the wood from early morning to about one o'clock in the afternoon. Then he would study for the rest of the day in a cabin which he and another young fellow shared, keeping house and cooking their own meals. It was during this period that Robert made up his mind that he wanted to be a mechanic. The year on the farm gave him the opportunity to settle the question of the kind of work he wanted to do and he resolved to educate himself along the lines of mathematics and engineering. By the time the year was up he had several hundred dollars in the bank, his savings on his wood-splitting contract, and had completed his correspondence school course in trigonometry and geometry.

Thus at nineteen years old, tall, powerfully built, the embodiment of physical health and strength, overflowing with the will and energy that seek release in long hours of hard work, an educational background which consisted of no more than the eighth grade of public school and a correspondence school course, a born-again Christian believer of unclarified aims, what might not God do with a life such as this? What did the great Master Mechanic have in store for His youthful *protegé*? It will be interesting to watch him at a few of his early preoccupations and observe the working out of the will of God in a life yielded to the divine Will but not as yet consecrated to the divine Purpose.

III

A Broken Neck

THE NEXT TEN YEARS of Robert LeTourneau's life were spent in Stockton, California,
roughly from 1908 to 1917. They were a sort of a
standing still period in his life, in which the Lord
waited for him to decide upon his walk. They were
years not without interest on the human side also, for
his father and mother moved to Stockton from Portland during this period and in Stockton Robert met
and married the young lady who is now Mrs. R. G.
LeTourneau. In fact, Stockton is important in this
history for several other reasons, namely, it was where
he made his own first home, where he lost his first
child and where the other six children were born,
and where the LeTourneau business as it exists today
was first established and is still being carried on.

These early years in Stockton were important in
still another way; they explain something of his
knowledge and skill as a mechanic which became the
groundwork of his success as a machinery manufacturer. It is interesting to point out that although he
was an ironworker by trade, he soon became a con-

vert to welding, and now uses no castings in his machines.

While he was still on the farm he possessed himself of a motorcycle and made a first-hand acquaintance with an internal combustion engine. He learned to take it apart and put it together again. Leaving the farm, he sought a job in a garage as a mechanic and after a short period of experience at this work, he and another young man decided to go into business for themselves. They pooled their resources and went into the automobile repair business, LeTourneau as mechanic and repair man, and his partner as salesman. The enterprise lasted for ten years. Referring to these days, he said, "People called me the man with two torches—one in each hand. I used to weld broken automobile frames, crankcases, and everything else, with my acetylene torches."

It was at this time he "took to welding," to quote his own words, and made some of the discoveries which played their part in his later success. From using his oxyacetylene torch to repair broken parts of cars and trucks, he made successful experiments in the building of shop fixtures and tools by the welding process. He discovered that welding enabled him to make designs which simplified work and cut costs, and that welded structures, built of steel, were exceptionally light, strong and rigid. There were no "blow-holes" to contend with, as with castings, and machining was simpler and less expensive. Welding, he found, permitted him to build things in a hurry, at a fraction of the time and cost required by other methods.

However, these discoveries of a technical and mechanical nature were not the only ones young LeTourneau made during his first business venture. He liked going places as well as figuring things out. That was true then as it is true today.

One of his experiences was a motorcycle trip to Portland, Oregon. Stockton to Portland in those days was a distance of eight hundred miles over roads which, compared with the roads of today, were pretty poor. His machine had no lights, so that he could ride only by day. The towns were far apart, the roads through the mountains steep, the pavements either rough or heavy with clay—the clay sticky enough to lock his wheels and make steering almost impossible. He found he could often do better riding alongside the road. He was doing pretty well at this on one occasion, when, without warning, he struck a rock, dived over the handlebars, and came down on the landscape with great suddenness and force—bruised but without serious injury.

Leaving his motorcycle, he climbed a hill to reconnoiter, and spied a farm house about a mile away, which he set out for. On the way he crossed a field in which a herd of western cattle were grazing. Brought up in dairy country, he thought these cattle to be friendly domestic cows. They turned out to be unfriendly steers. They started for him at once. Still thinking they were only cows, he picked up a ten-

foot rail from a near-by fence and brandished his way
through them—almost. Realizing at last that he had
wild steers to deal with and that the herd was several
times larger than he had at first thought, he pulled
out a revolver which a friend had lent him for self-
protection on his journey and fired several shots into
the air. It scattered some of the steers nearest to him
and permitted him to escape over a fence.

He reached Portland at last, wiser in many ways
about steers, mechanical transportation, mountain
roads, and many other things.

Many times since his conversion, Robert LeTourneau has had miraculous deliverances from physical
harm, and even from death. These deliverances have
been due, he has always declared, to the unremitting
guardianship of his heavenly Father.

One day, while welding some broken parts together in a pit under a car, and fearing the flame of
his torch might ignite the grease with which the parts
were covered, he called to a bystander to be ready
with a pail of water. The bystander, it happened, was
a personal friend and the man after whom he was
named, Robert Gilmour. The flame from the torch
did ignite the grease, Robert yelled for the water, and
the bystander threw the contents of the pail in the
direction of the burning grease. The contents of the
pail turned out to be gasoline, which exploded with a
roar. Robert leaped from under the car, rushed to the
garage a hundred feet away, seized a fire extinguisher,
and put out the fire without much damage to the car

and none to himself. That his escape from death on this occasion was miraculous he verily believes.

Automobile racing interested Robert during those days in Stockton. Speed seems to be ingrained in his nature. A newspaper reporter once said of him, "He's a wack on speed." His interest in it at that time, however, almost cost him his life.

Robert was one day trying out a racing car when his car lost a wheel while going at a high rate of speed. The car left the track and plunged through eight sections of barbed-wire and board fence. Unconscious for forty-eight hours, he came to in a hospital room, exclaiming as he glanced at the window and then at the nurse, "Where did I get those curtains?" and "Where did you come from?" His neck was broken. For two months his head lay useless on his shoulder. Then he recovered and the only trace of that accident today is a slight tilt in the way he carries his head.

Thus he occupied himself and thus the years passed until 1917.

Eager to serve his country in the World War, Robert left his garage business in the hands of his partner and entered the machine shop at Mare Island Navy Yard, San Francisco Bay, remaining there until the signing of the Armistice, the year and the month in which he reached his thirtieth birthday. He went back to Stockton and the garage business, only to find that things were in pretty bad shape. After six months' effort to straighten things out he and his partner found themselves owing about $5000, with nothing with which to pay the creditors. So they closed up the business and Robert started out to look for a job by means of which he might earn money to pay his debts.

A friend met him on the street one day and asked him what he was going to do. He said he would take the first job that came along and didn't care what kind of a job it was. The friend told him he could get him a job on the "islands," a locality well known to people who live in Stockton, overhauling some tractors, but in order to get the job he would have to demonstrate his ability as a mechanic by repairing a boat engine which was generally considered by every one who knew about it to be unrepairable. Robert repaired the boat engine and secured the tractor job, which was on a large farm in the San Joaquin Valley.

He was shown an old 75 tractor and told to overhaul it and make it run. When he got it to running he was told to take it over to a forty-acre piece of land and level it with a scraper. He finished the job and wondered whether leveling land wasn't a pretty good business for him to get into. But he couldn't go into it without a tractor and a scraper and he had no money. He consulted a banker acquaintance. The banker approved his plan and agreed to back him in the purchase of a 75 Holt tractor and a scraper. He started out as a contractor. He hadn't gone very far when he saw that his scraper wasn't constructed as he thought it should be. So he got out his acetylene torch, procured some steel, and built himself a scraper.

He said of it, "It worked pretty good. After I'd been using it awhile, a fellow came up and said he wanted me to make one for him. I told him to take mine and I would build another for myself. When I built the second one I corrected some of the things I knew were wrong with the first one." That was the way it started. He kept building scrapers, and other contractors bought them as fast as he built them, and he kept improving them. All the scrapers on the market were riveted and he believed that welded construction was more serviceable and lasting. This was in 1920.

LeTourneau was thirty-two. Sixteen years had gone by since his conversion—two years in foundries, a year on a farm, ten years in a garage, two years at Mare Island, and another year since. He had been a Christian for sixteen years. He knew he was saved and on his way to heaven but he felt that nothing that he did counted for Jesus Christ. Many times during this period his younger sister would say to him, "Bob, don't you love Jesus?" He knew that she had something in her heart—a love that he did not have. She had a passion for souls and wanted to tell everyone about the Lord she loved. She went to China as a missionary. These reflections gave Robert much concern. He knew that he had been living an aimless Christian life for sixteen years.

A revival campaign was on in Stockton and Robert attended the meetings. A call was extended for consecrated lives. Robert went forward. He knelt and prayed, "Lord, I know my Christian life has been a failure. I haven't been living for You. I have tried to turn over a new leaf, but it just seems I can't make the grade. I have been ashamed of You." He said that as he knelt there he realized what a coward he had been. He cried out from the depths of his soul, "Lord, if You will give me a victorious Christian life and put the love in my heart that I know ought to be there and fill me with Your Spirit so that I can witness for You, I'll do whatever you ask me to do from this day on."

He said, "God heard my cry while I was on my knees. I didn't have to wait until the next day to know whether I was accepted. I arose from my knees with the determination to keep my promise. The next morning I went to see the pastor and told him, 'Brother, God did something for me last night and I promised Him I would do anything He wants me to do from this day on.' I had an idea that in order to serve God I would have to be a preacher or a missionary, and that He might send me out as a missionary. I didn't see how it could be done, but now I was willing, while before that I had not been. I said to the pastor, 'Do you think God wants me to be a missionary?' He said, 'Let's pray about it.' So we both knelt down and prayed. When we arose from our knees, he said these words to me—they still ring in my ears as the voice of God speaking to my soul—'God needs business men as well as missionaries.' I answered, 'I will do my best to be God's business man.'"

Ever since that moment Robert LeTourneau has been trying to carry out that commission. The events of his life from that hour bear convincing testimony to the sincerity and success of his efforts. He believes that if every business man could realize the opportunity he has to serve God in his business, the world and business would be far different and better. He believes that God has a place for every one, in business, in the workshop, in the home, behind the sacred desk, on the foreign field, and that every one is happiest when he finds that place. He said recently, "I am still trying to be God's business man. That is why we hold gospel meetings wherever He leads. I wouldn't trade places with anyone. I am happy in the service of the King. If only people would know the joy and satisfaction and peace that come from this service, they would say, 'Lord, here am I. Take me and make me what You want me to be.' "

He said, "From the minute I made God my business partner, things started to go."

He began his career as a land-leveling contractor and immediately began building scrapers, so that he was a manufacturer almost from the time he became a contractor. He spent his evenings designing bigger and more powerful scrapers and his days in constructing them and in carrying out his road-building and other land-leveling contracts. His success in designing and building these machines enabled him to take contracts at lower figures than such work had formerly been done for and led to more and more demand for his services and his machines. As fast as he built new scrapers, he sold his old ones to other contractors. His "shop" was the open field beside his home.

In 1921 Robert built his own manufacturing plant in Stockton, known as the "old Moss Avenue Shop," which is still standing. A year later he made his first "drag scraper," and later in the same year his first "gondola." Here, too, he built his first "mountain mover" and other large-capacity scrapers, which gained recognition throughout the West for their dirt-moving economy.

The years from 1921 to 1929 were years of struggle. It was a small business—at the beginning a local business. Because it was a combined contracting and manufacturing business one department hampered the other. A big contract tied up all the equipment and held up manufacturing. At the same time, the experiences of the contracting business led to the building of better machines. The business grew steadily during these years, but the growth was slow. There were many setbacks, many obstacles to be overcome, many lessons to be learned. By 1930 the capacity of the Moss Avenue shop was outgrown and a new plant of welded steel construction, 60 by 300 feet in size, was erected on Roosevelt Street and Wilson Way in Stockton. The business was incorporated in 1929—R. G. LeTourneau, Inc., a California corporation.

The eleven years from 1920 to 1930 saw Robert LeTourneau changed from an employee to an em-

ployer, from an unknown mechanic working for wages
to the head of his own business, with sometimes large
numbers of men working for him. Many of these
men are still with him, holding responsible positions.
Little did he dream, even at forty-two, what God had
in store for him in the next eleven years. But there
were many testings ahead.

IV

Working on Sunday

A FAVORITE SAYING of Robert LeTourneau's is, "The trouble with most of us is that we try to fit God into our plans rather than fit ourselves into *His* plan." One of the first mistakes he made after he decided to make God his business partner was in the matter of money. In referring to this mistake he recently said, "At that time I kept saying to myself, 'Next year I will have a lot of money for the Lord. I will be true to Him later.' I did not know that *now* is the Lord's time. To Him the 'first fruits.' That is why we call our shop paper 'NOW.' If God speaks to your heart tonight, *now* is the time. Don't put it off. When it came to giving, I thought I won't pledge so much this year. Next year I will have more to give. But next year we were facing bankruptcy."

Two experiences were involved in this crisis. The first of these occurred about the year 1931. Two large construction projects were in hand. The first was a million-dollar contract to build a highway to Boulder Dam on the Colorado River in Nevada. The second was a half-million-dollar contract to build the Orange County Dam in Southern California. Unexpected difficulties in completing the Boulder Dam highway contract left LeTourneau with a loss of $100,000.

This heavy loss made it impossible to undertake the second contract without outside financial help. A bonding company in San Francisco would do either one of two things, they would take the contract out of LeTourneau's hands, or furnish the necessary finances and appoint an overseer to superintend the work and safeguard the interests of the company. The latter course was decided upon as the only possible way to recover the loss incurred in completing the first contract.

The overseer of the bonding company, when he appeared on the scene, hindered more than he helped. He endeavored to tell LeTourneau how to run things. To make matters worse, a State inspector appeared about the same time. He said, "You are too late getting started. The rainy season will be here and wash out what you do with loss of life and property. We can't let you go ahead; you will have to wait until next year." He had the authority, under California law, to carry out the threat implied by his words. In Southern California there is no rain in summer. Work on highways and similar projects must be done before the rains start. The inspector said, "You can-not get this work done before fall." LeTourneau argued. The loss involved in abandoning the work with the men and equipment on the job meant a loss beyond hope of financial recovery. The inspector relented: "I'll tell you what you can do. There are

400,000 cubic yards to be built into the base of this dam which can be put in without danger to life or property. If you can complete that foundation in one month, I know you'll be able to do the rest on time."

Such an undertaking looked impossible. LeTourneau had planned on 200,000 cubic yards for the first month. He discussed it with his men. He had a small force, but they realized it was the only hope for the company's existence. They said, "Let's try it." They worked days and nights and Sundays. Extra machines were put in. The wheels never stopped turning.

When the month was up and the figures in, the goal was achieved, with a good margin of safety. Nothing like it had ever been accomplished before. With the foundation completed, what remained to be done on the contract would be finished within the specified time, working at the same rate of speed—day and night and Sunday.

LeTourneau had not been in the habit of working his men on Sunday, although it was common practice in the contracting business, especially where time and weather conditions had to be taken into account, to work seven days a week. Sunday was a convenient day for making repairs to equipment and machines. But working on Sunday troubled Robert's conscience. He felt it was not God's way. Besides, an evangelist was holding Sunday meetings in a near-by town, and he wanted to attend those meetings with as many of his crew as wanted to go with him.

He approached the bonding company's overseer: "I

want to stop this Sunday work. My men have worked hard this past month. With one day's rest each week, they'll accomplish as much work in six days as they would by working seven."

The overseer replied: "Not on your life. If you don't work seven days a week, we'll take over the job."

LeTourneau prayed, "Lord, what can I do?" A still small Voice within him said, "Obey God rather than man." He went to his foremen on Saturday night and issued orders that there would be no work on Sunday. On Sunday morning just two men showed up—the overseer and his assistant.

When the crew resumed work on Monday morning, a furious overseer telephoned the main office of the bonding company.

"What's the big idea?" shouted the head man at San Francisco when he got LeTourneau on the telephone. "We try to help you out and this is the way you turn us down. You know what that means! Work on Sunday, or we take over and you're out." To which LeTourneau answered, "I cannot change my decision. You can take everything I have except my wife and children."

Knowing in his heart God was able to save his business, he prayed again, "Lord, give me faith."

Three days later the head of the bonding company arrived on the scene. He walked up to LeTourneau and put out his hand. "Go ahead with the job," he said, "and I will stand back of you."

UPPER. Mr. and Mrs. R. G. LeTourneau and their six children. Extreme right, Donald Philip, oldest son.

LOWER. LeTourneau family's new steel home about two minutes from plant and airport, Toccoa.

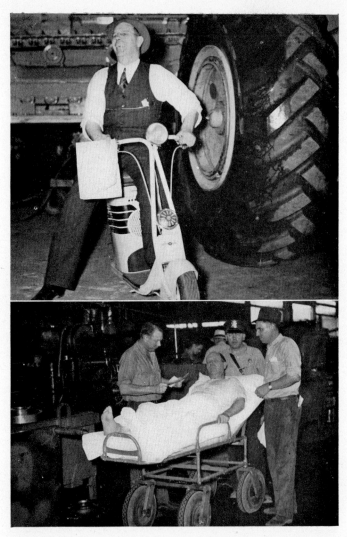

UPPER. R. G. on scooter, saves time in getting about Peoria and Toccoa plants.
LOWER. Robert, after auto accident, convalesced on portable cot in
factory.

Said LeTourneau later: "I don't know what changed his mind, for I never asked him. I feel sure that what he said to me wasn't in his mind when he left San Francisco. Something happened to him on that journey. God dealt with him."

The contract was completed on time without Sunday work. It seemed as if the machinery was no longer in need of repairs on Saturday night. The profit earned by the company when the work was finished put it in a more solvent condition.

The second of the experiences referred to at the outset of this chapter occurred in 1932. Of this experience LeTourneau said:

"It was the beginning of the business depression. I found myself with debts amounting to several hundreds of thousands of dollars. Many firms in better shape than ours was, went down, never to rise again. The pay roll was about five weeks behind. We had stalled the material men until we couldn't hold them off much longer. My attorney said to me, 'You cannot go any farther. You must appoint a receiver. The papers are made out and should be filed today.' I did not know what was going to happen. I said, 'Wait a few days longer.' The next day was Sunday and the closing of our missionary convention.

"I sat in the choir. Our people were making their pledges for missions. God spoke to my heart, 'How about making a pledge for missions this year?' I said, 'Lord, how can I?' In the congregation I saw a number of young men who worked in my factory. They

had had no pay for five weeks. If I made my custo-
mary pledge, the amount would be announced, and
everybody would know it was my pledge. They would
call me a hypocrite for making a pledge for missions
when I wasn't paying my bills. I prayed, 'Lord, what
shall I do?' A still small Voice said, 'Divide your
pledge and make it in the names of your children.
Put Me on your payroll and pay Me when you pay the
others.' I obeyed and made the pledge. When I told
our bookkeeper what I had done and that my missionary pledge of $5000 had to be listed with the other
obligations, she threw up her hands, for she had been
ordered to pay $25 per $5000 of indebtedness to our
creditors in order to forestall receivership and bankruptcy. I told her, 'The missionary pledge must be
paid first.' She said, 'Then you might as well give up.'

"Just about this time I had brought out a new
machine and had sold it to a contractor on condition
that it would work satisfactorily for him. It was bigger
than any machine I had previously built. He telephoned me, 'This machine is too big and heavy and
won't work in this desert sand.' I said, 'I'll send you
a smaller machine.' He said, 'No. Even your smaller
machine is too big for the work I have here—the
tractor won't pull it. I'll find what I need elsewhere.'

"In desperation, I remembered that about a year
before I had purchased a set of the largest pneumatic
tires then obtainable, thinking they would work more
satisfactorily than steel tires on tractor-drawn machines, although I had never been able to induce any

contractor to try, much less buy, a scraper thus equipped. I still had these pneumatics and they gave me an idea.

" 'Listen!' I said, 'I have a set of pneumatic tires which I am going to put on that smaller scraper and tow it by truck to your place of business. This is permissible under road regulations and will cost you nothing for freight. If the scraper does not work, I'll have my driver bring it back without cost to you.' I convinced him it was worth a trial.

"When the test was made, he called me up and said, 'The small scraper is going like a house afire. Send me the steel wheels that belong to it.'

"This was something I didn't want to do, fearful the steel wheels would not work on his job. But I sent them with a heavy heart. When the steel wheels arrived, he took off two of the pneumatics from the rear of the small scraper, put the steel wheels on in their place, then put these two pneumatics on the front end of the big scraper, and ran both scrapers out on the grade for a test. The big scraper ran one speed faster than the small scraper.

"Surprised at this performance, the contractor called me on the telephone: 'Come down on the night train.' When I arrived, he said: 'I'll buy this small scraper with the pneumatic tires. I also want a full set of pneumatics for the big scraper. Then I want another big scraper with pneumatics all around.' I said, 'Wait a minute. I have only built one of those big scrapers.' He replied, 'Well, can't you build another?' 'Yes,' I answered, 'but I'm short of money. If you could let me have a small down payment in advance—' 'Down payment!' he exclaimed. 'I'll write you a check for the whole amount right now!' "

Robert LeTourneau returned to his factory with a check for $25,000 in his pocket, a sum sufficient to cover his missionary pledge and make substantial payments to his creditors. The sale he made of scrapers equipped with pneumatic tires instead of steel wheels marked an innovation in the construction of tractor-drawn machines and has since come into general use by all makers of heavy grading equipment.

That God worked throughout both of the experiences described in this chapter to the preservation of the business into which He had been taken as a partner, and that His hand definitely guided His servant in the course he followed, there has never been any question in Robert's mind. He proved that "God will not be any man's debtor." He said, "I failed the Lord when I said, 'It will take all my finances to handle the program I have set this year, and next year I'll have a lot of money for the Lord.' But I was wrong. It doesn't take much faith to count up what's left and give God a portion of it. God expects us to let Him have the first fruits and trust Him that the harvest will be sufficient to meet the needs, for without faith we are told it is impossible to please Him. What a wonderful God we have! Why don't we believe Him more?"

When injustice and self-interest unexpectedly intrude themselves between the Christian and his Lord, there is a sifting of the soul by Satan such as led Peter to deny his Master with an oath. Something like such a sifting of the soul came to Robert LeTourneau when a man with whom he had earned a large profit on a contract claimed it all; and again when an urgent business engagement stood between him and attendance at a Gospel meeting. How these situations arose, how they were dealt with, and the consequences to the man whose career is here described, is next to be recounted.

V

On Going to Law

ONE of the severest testings in his life came to Robert during the period in which, with the Lord as his partner, he was laying the foundation of his business.

He had been engaged in highway construction work for some time when, as he says, "I got my eyes on a piece of State highway construction which was a little too big for me to handle with the equipment and men I then had." In his church was another man who had had experience in highway construction work, a Christian, whose equipment, added to Robert's, would be equal to the handling of the contract. He sought this man out and suggested to him that they bid for the work "as partners." They did so and secured the contract.

Shortly after the work was undertaken, difficulties revealed themselves. The work was tough, the inspector was tougher, progress was slow, and it began to look as though they might lose some money on the contract. Robert's associate was one of the worrying kind. He began to find fault with one thing after another and finally said to Robert, "The trouble with this job is that you have too many of your own relatives working for you."

The charge concerning his relatives was true to the extent that he did have a lot of them working for him. But he maintained that they were all "doing their stuff" and he didn't want to lay them off as skilled labor was not always available when it was needed and he thought he would have work for all of them on future contracts after the present one had been completed.

As was his custom when in doubt about God's will for him in a situation, he went to prayer. He asked God to show him what to do. It is one of Robert's convictions that when a child of God is doing the best he can, he has a right to ask the Lord to help him; but he does not believe in telling the Lord to bring it on a silver platter. Therefore, he prayed and things began to happen.

He got an invitation to bid on another contract from a private concern which never sent out public bids. The execution of this contract, like the State highway job he was handling with his fellow church member, would require machinery that he didn't have. He went to his machinery manufacturer and asked for credit. He got the credit and entered his bid. He and two other contractors were within a few cents of one another with their bids, and Robert, thinking he was unknown and without prestige and therefore hardly in the running, was happily surprised to be awarded the contract.

He went back to his State highway construction job and transferred every one of his relatives to the new contract, appointing his brother-in-law as superintendent. They went through with it according to schedule and made a nice profit. Not long thereafter the State highway job was completed, and contrary to expectations, there was a nice profit on that too. With the profits made on both contracts, all of Robert's obligations to creditors could have been met. But his human "partner" on the State highway job had a different idea.

His idea was that because Robert had made a profit on the second contract, all of the profit on the State highway contract should go to the "partner." That profit was $40,000, and it was to have been split $20,000 to each.

Stunned by the stark unreasonableness of such a proposal from a Christian and fellow church member, Robert went to see his lawyer. His lawyer told him, "Don't worry. He hasn't a leg to stand on." But he did worry—for a different reason. Not because he feared he couldn't collect in court but because the man and he, besides being Christians and members of the same church, were both on the official board of that church. What would happen to the church if two of its leading members should engage in a lawsuit? He was familiar with the Scripture which forbade brother going to law with brother but thought he knew how to work it so that the other man would be the one to go to law and that he could persuade more people in the church to side with him than with his erstwhile "partner." Robert often says of himself at this time, "I was not exactly lamblike of disposition. I liked to take the bull by the horns. I said, 'Lord, that money belongs to my creditors. I've got to pay them.'" Then the Lord spoke to his heart: "How much do you love Me? How much do you love My people? How much do you love My church?"

Robert did what he has confessed was the hardest thing he ever did in his life. He went to that man and said: "Brother, we're not going to have a lawsuit over this thing. If you insist upon having all of the profit, you can have it. If the Lord doesn't want you to have it, He can take it away from you. If He wants me to have my share, He can give it to me." He thought by saying this it might cause the man to change his mind. It didn't. He took the entire profit and Robert let him have it.

A short time after this incident, that man went out and secured another contract. And a short time after, Robert secured another contract. On the contract which he took the other man lost the entire $40,000, while Robert made enough on his contract to make up for the profit he had sacrificed. In his own words: "I proved that it pays to obey God." A favorite expression with him is: "Don't obey God because it pays, for then it won't pay. But obey Him because you love Him, and then it will pay."

Another severe testing that came along about this

time, and the way in which he met it, was to have far-reaching consequences in his business.

During these Stockton days the business was small, employing about a dozen men. A piece of work of considerable importance was in the shop and had to be completed on the following day. One vital part for this machine was needed which had not yet been designed. It was not until the end of the day that Robert realized his men would have to start on the making of that important part the first thing on the following morning in order to complete the work next day. Unless the design was laid out and ready for them when they came to work, it would be impossible for them to begin the building of the part. Up to that moment, he had not the slightest idea what the designing of the part involved or how long it would take him to work it out. There was nothing else for him to do but spend the evening over his drafting board with slide rule and pencil.

Suddenly he realized he had another engagement for that evening. It was the evening upon which a group of young people of the church took charge of the meeting in a certain gospel mission of the town and he had promised his Lord to accompany them and do his part in the service of song and testimony. He said, "Lord, I can't go to the mission tonight. I've got to figure this thing out." The still small Voice he knew so well said to him, "Did you mean it when you promised to serve Me no matter what the cost?"

The temptation to skip the mission service, more-over, was intensified by the reflection that he was not on the program for any special part in the service and that the young people would be able to get along very well without him. The struggle was a hard one, although, as he said later, it should not have been. At length, he said: "All right, Lord; I'll go. I don't know what I'll do tomorrow, but I'll go. I promised I would and I will."

He went to the mission meeting and returned home about ten o'clock. His home was not far from the plant. Thinking of the part which had to be designed, he began to wonder what he ought to do. The thought of trying to design anything that night didn't appeal to him because he felt his mind ought to be fresh and alert to work out the thing which he wanted to be an original and effective part of the machine. Such things are not done, he felt, when the mind is half awake. The more he thought of it, the more hopeless it seemed.

Becoming more and more concerned, he went to the plant and sat down at his drafting board. He hadn't been there ten minutes before the entire design flashed before his mind's eye, complete and perfect. He made his calculations, put them on paper, and left his instructions for the men to start the work of making the unit when they came to work in the morning. Then he went to bed.

The design which Robert LeTourneau worked out in about ten minutes' time that night after he re-

turned from the mission is the vital part of the main
control unit with which all machines made by the
company are equipped from that day to the present.
The far-reaching significance of LeTourneau's invention that night is revealed in the following story:

A number of years after the incident described,
LeTourneau salesmen from all parts of the world met
at the company's annual sales meeting in Peoria.
Many of them were much concerned over news that
had just been received that a very large company—
ten times larger than the LeTourneau company at
that time—was to be a competitor, having just put out
a machine similar to the machines made by LeTourneau. A long discussion ensued in which some uneasi-
ness manifested itself among the salesmen until a few
of them, who had seen the competing machine, explained that its power control unit was in no way to
be compared with the power control unit of the
LeTourneau machine.

At the company banquet that evening, Mr. LeTourneau was asked to speak. Knowing of what had happened at the sales meeting, and thinking to bring
home to the group, and particularly to those who
were not Christians, the practical value of faith in
God to all who accept salvation as it is in Jesus Christ,
he retold the story of the mission meeting and the
tangible reward which God had given him in the
shape of the design of the power control unit. Several of the men present were of the group of work-

men who had waited for Robert to work out that design. There was a hushed silence as he said:

"You sat around discussing our competitor's machine and found out there was one thing about it which puts it out of the running with our product. I'm here to tell you that the one feature which lifts it out of competition is the unit I designed the night I returned from the mission. God help us to believe and put His will into our hearts."

Many practical answers to prayer were vouchsafed to Robert LeTourneau during the building up of his business in Stockton. From nothing at all the business grew steadily to annual sales of hundreds of thousands of dollars. His story of how his faith in God enabled him to develop that business into national and then to international proportions, and to increase sales to millions of dollars annually, is a still more enthralling story, as interesting to the skeptic as to the Christian believer.

VI

Peoria is Taken

THE GREATEST business depression ever experienced in the United States was ushered in by the spectacular stock market crash of November 1929. About three weeks after this commercial cataclysm rocked the country and before the effects of it were being felt in California, Robert LeTourneau incorporated his business. On November 19, 1929, a $100,000 combination manufacturing and contracting business was incorporated under the name R. G. Le-Tourneau, Inc., of Stockton, California.

In 1929 the company comprised about twenty men. Many operations were performed by hand in those days, such as the forming of steel disks with a fifty-pound sledge. Annual sales of land-leveling machinery, sold for use mostly in the western States, were less than $100,000. Sales and earnings since incorporation of the Stockton business are shown on opposite page.

From a shed in 1920 and a small local business to annual sales of close to a million dollars in 1934 covered a period of fourteen years, a sort of coming-of-age period in which the enterprise experienced its

Year	Sales	Net Profits
1930	$110,808.60	$34,474.92
1931	155,345.08	32,507.41 (Loss)
1932	207,236.81	52,055.61
1933	379,106.53	113,092.27
1934	929,860.67	340,275.49

PRAISE GOD!

"growing up" pains. The man at the head of the business was now forty-six.

Glancing backward for a moment, in order to more clearly understand one of the important business reasons which led LeTourneau to establish a new plant in another part of the country far from the original location, the student of industrial development sees him first as a "land-leveling contractor." The record says he *bought* his first tractor but *built* his first scraper, because he wanted a better scraper than the market afforded at that time and wanted it at less cost. As it has already been pointed out, scrapers then on the market were *riveted*. Robert wanted a *welded* scraper, believing that welded construction was more efficient and serviceable. And the only way to get what he wanted was to build it himself.

Robert's first "factory" was put up and occupied in 1921, the old Moss Avenue shop, and served the steadily expanding business until 1930, when a new welded steel plant, 60 by 300 feet in size, was erected on Roosevelt Street and Wilson Way. In 1934 this plant was enlarged to 140 by 340 feet. Meantime, demand for the machines made by the manufacturing department of the business absorbed all of the company's facilities and the contracting department was thereupon liquidated.

LeTourneau scrapers and dirt-hauling machines are for the most part tractor-drawn. LeTourneau did not manufacture tractors. Of the various makes on the market, those made by the Caterpillar Tractor Company, Peoria, Illinois, because of their "track-type" design and greater power in hauling heavy equipment of the LeTourneau type, were found to be as generally satisfactory, and more so in some respects, than other makes. For this and other important reasons, Robert decided to expand his business eastward and build a factory in Peoria.

With characteristic enterprise the site was purchased, freight cars were loaded in Stockton with tools and equipment, and the small company of pioneers from California descended upon Peoria one rainy morning in the spring of 1935. Robert and his associates, trudging down the right-of-way of the Rock Island Railroad through the rain and murk to gaze upon the muddy field which was to be the future Peoria factory, must have had plenty of courage, faith, and a rare quality of imagination. It rained all week. When they arrived there was not even a siding upon which to switch their freight cars—not even a shed into which their tools and equipment might be unloaded.

To tell a man of Robert LeTourneau's temperament, "You can't do that!" is the surest way to get

UPPER. Dorothy M. Strathearn, known as "The Gospel Nightingale," who regularly sings on programs with Mr. LeTourneau.

LOWER. Carolina Gospel Quartet, popular colored singers on many LeTourneau programs.

UPPER. LeTourneau Hall, at Toccoa Falls Institute, Toccoa Falls,
Ga., "Where Character is Developed with Intellect."
LOWER. First factory building at Toccoa, Ga., dedicated July 11,
1939.

him into action. The task before him in Peoria might have discouraged a man less gifted with his peculiar talent for invention, exploration, and accomplishing the impossible. A factory had to be planned and erected, a railroad siding put in, receiving and shipping facilities provided for, machines and equipment purchased and installed, other equipment built, labor employed, and a thousand other minor and major problems solved. He rolled up his sleeves and said to his associates, "All right. Let's get going!"

Within a month the siding was in, the foundation for a 60-by-300-foot factory was laid out and building started, an "open-air" production system was in operation, a twelve-ton traveling crane was devised and built, steel storage racks, handling equipment, tools, jigs, fixtures, and other production equipment was installed, and in addition to all this, the manufacturing force turned out thirteen big scrapers.

The speed with which Robert LeTourneau works is due in large degree to his belief in, and wide-scale use of, welding in his manufacturing operations. For the past ten years he has not used a casting or a rivet in any manufacturing process, and in one year he turned out well over 25,000 tons of finished product. Another manufacturer of industrial equipment said of that remarkable thirty-day accomplishment at Peoria:

"The work of that spring month in 1935 was by no means a flash in the pan. Without changing pace, LeTourneau and his organization kept going.

During that first month the sparks of the welding arc were flying even before the bending brakes, shears, templates, and other equipment, were unloaded from the siding, and one of the first pieces of equipment built was an ingenious unloading crane which Le-Tourneau sketched out on a piece of paper one afternoon at three o'clock, and by the next day it was in operation.

"With LeTourneau, welding is a *thinking* tool as well as a manufacturing and construction tool. It simplifies invention. It gives him engineering freedom to devise new and valuable design ideas that vastly improve existing practices. Many designers are handicapped, he says, because they think in terms of castings. When they redesign to get the greater strength and uniformity of rolled steel, they try to convert the old casting into a welding. The most effective approach is to forget all about former methods. To be successful with welding, think in terms of welding and follow the rules of welding just as the castings man thinks in terms of castings and follows the rules of castings."

The general who knows where the enemy is going to be next and "gits thar fust" has a better chance of winning. Likewise, the speed with which a ball team gets into action often piles up runs and points at the very outset which win games. The progress made in that first spring month of 1935 set a pace that broke records before the year was ended. In the winter of that first year the company found it necessary to add another 300 feet to the plant in order to take care of increasing business. A year later, 600 feet more were added to make the plant 1200 feet long. In 1937 the factory was enlarged to a steel-and-glass structure 160 feet wide by nearly a quarter of a mile long—a $13,000,000 plant with 1200 men on the payroll. At the same time improvement in the design and construction of LeTourneau products for better service and more economical operation enabled the company to effect economies in its own manufacturing operations and lower costs. An interesting by-product of the business is the fabrication of all-steel arc-welded houses, designed by LeTourneau as dwellings for the use of officers and employees of the company. They were first used for temporary offices in Peoria. These houses are of modernistic design, attractive appearance, and are convenient and comfortable to live in, and inexpensive to build. Close to the Peoria plant is a community consisting of twenty-three of these steel fabricated houses, each completely air-conditioned for winter and summer.

The record of sales and earnings of the Stockton and Peoria plants of R. G. LeTourneau, Inc., for the four years from 1935 to 1938 follow:

Year	Sales	Net Profits
1935	$2,004,595.86	$ 586,377.75
1936	4,392,402.68	1,364,393.41
1937	5,674,305.24	1,262,540.87
1938	6,246,846.05	1,412,465.68

A "dedication" service marked the opening of the new steel-and-glass factory at Peoria in 1937. Robert LeTourneau believes that a factory may be dedicated to the Lord as truly as a church. Upon the occasion of the Peoria plant dedication, he spoke as follows:

"Some people may wonder what religion has to do with business. A number of years ago I asked myself the question, 'What's the use of having a religion that doesn't work?' The Spirit of the Lord spoke to me and I realized that while I professed to love the Lord Jesus Christ, my actions didn't prove it. I professed to have a Saviour Who was able to help me and at the same time I went worrying along in my own strength.

"I said to myself, 'If God is what I claim He is, why not go into partnership with Him?' I got down on my knees and made a deal with God. I feel I could have kept my part of the deal much better than I have. But this business and its unparalleled growth shows that God has done His part. A few years ago my creditors were trying to decide whether to give us a chance to pay up or take their loss on the Le-Tourneau account. Now we are dedicating the second addition to our eastern factory and doubling our production capacity in an effort to keep up with orders.

"You see, we have a personal God, a personal Saviour. Isn't it marvelous that He is willing to condescend to make a personal deal with you and me, the creatures of His hand? If I did not seek to give God the glory and tell the world that this business really belongs to Him, seeking to honor Him in the dedication of this splendid new building, I would not be fulfilling my part of the deal.

"On the other hand, I would not seek to lower His grace to the level of a bargain. The Lord Jesus Christ, in the shedding of His precious blood to wash away our sins, has done that which we can never repay. The Lord of glory left the ivory palaces and came down to this world of woe—'that though He was rich, yet for your sakes He became poor, that ye through His poverty might be rich.' When we look at it from that angle, we must admit that no mortal would ever be able to repay Him. But because I believe that God wants business men, as well as preachers, to be His servants, I believe that a factory can be dedicated to His service as well as a church, and that it can be the means of saving many souls.

"I believe that the world is looking for a religion that really works, and while I realize that success is not always measured in dollars and cents, any more than true joy and happiness can be measured that way, I am certain that if those who profess the name of Christ would really put their confidence in Him, they would find that God would not fail them."

Still another addition to the Peoria plant, size 132 by 284 feet, was similarly dedicated on March 10-15, 1940. For the dedication services, the new building was used as a temporary auditorium with seats arranged for six thousand people. Many widely known speakers were on the program and delivered stirring gospel messages. One service was given over to the relief of war-torn Finland. Ex-President Herbert Hoover, national chairman of the Finnish Relief Fund, was the principal speaker. The meetings began on Sunday and ran through to Friday. The occasion attracted wide attention and representatives of the press reported the proceedings in generous space, invariably emphasizing the religious aspect. One newspaper went so far as to say that were all factories dedicated under such auspices, the history of America's commercial civilization might have been a vastly different story from what it has been.

In April, 1941, the buildings of the Avery Farm Machinery Co., Inc., adjacent to the LeTourneau plant in Peoria, were acquired, and have added 282,627 square feet to the company's manufacturing facilities in that city.

It is time to pause for a little while and turn back some of the pages in Robert LeTourneau's career. As well might an artist hope to paint a true likeness of a person without seeing that person as for a scribe to attempt to delineate a man's character and describe his accomplishments without telling his readers something about the most important human relationship in his life and presenting the person who constitutes the second half of that relationship—his wife.

VII

An Elopement

ROBERT'S father and mother, with their family of five boys and three girls, had moved from Portland, Oregon, to Stockton, California, in 1909, when Robert was twenty-one. Living also in Stockton at this time was the Peterson family. They had a daughter, Evelyn, who was about twelve years of age at this time. They both attended a little Sunday school in Stockton and there's where they first met.

In course of time a personal interest began to grow in the mind of each of these young people toward the other. When Robert's father and mother heard of it, not knowing the Petersons, they wondered whether the young lady about whom Robert was beginning to talk so much was the right sort of girl for him.

"Look here, my lad," said Robert's father one day, "that girl is not for you."

"You've got me wrong, Dad," answered Robert. "I'm not thinking seriously about her. I'm an automobile mechanic and too busy fixing cars all day to have time for anything else. We're just friends."

In all probability Robert thought he told his father

the truth. However that may be, about a year later, Mr. Peterson, Evelyn's father, showed his confidence in and regard for Robert in an unusual way. The firm for which Mr. Peterson worked had a strike. One day on the street a group of strikers and union sympathizers cornered Mr. Peterson and might have done him serious physical harm had he not eluded them and taken refuge in a near-by house. From this haven he telephoned to Robert to come and get him. The latter hopped into his racing car, sped to the scene, picked up Mr. Peterson and whisked him away to safety. For the next succeeding three or four days he called for him at his home, drove him to work, made sure he got there safely, and brought him back at night. Then Mr. Peterson invited Robert to come and make his home with the Peterson family. Mrs. Peterson seconded her husband's invitation and Robert accepted and moved in. Evelyn was about thirteen.

About two years later Robert went to Mr. Peterson and told him he wanted to marry Evelyn. No objection was offered. As to just when they would be married, however, nothing definite was decided upon, and matters drifted along for another year or more. Then Robert spoke to Mr. Peterson again. But the father said he felt that Evelyn was too young and that Robert ought to wait awhile. He waited as long as he could, which was several months, and once again brought the matter up, telling Mr. Peterson that in his—Robert's—opinion, Evelyn was plenty old enough. This time Mr. Peterson definitely said "No."

"I told him I had waited long enough," said Robert, "but he wouldn't listen to me. So I decided we would elope. Evelyn was willing. I felt sure it would be all right with Mrs. Peterson and that the only reason she had not given her consent to our getting married was for the sake of preserving peace in the family.

"So we eloped in my car and started for the Mexican border with Evelyn's father hot on the trail. But not for long. He soon gave up. We reached the border and were married in Mexico so that I would not have to tell an untruth about Evelyn's age. Her father was very angry because I had taken the matter into my own hands; and he tried to have the marriage annulled. He took the matter to the district attorney but the latter ruled that if our marriage was legal in Mexico it would have to be recognized in this country. Mr. Peterson carried the grudge against me for six years, refusing to be reconciled. At length he came to me and said, 'Let's bury the hatchet.' We did and were good friends till the day of his death many years later."

The marriage took place in Tia Juana, Mexico, on August 29, 1917.

Robert LeTourneau's Christian testimony has been recorded in this history, but how about Evelyn Peterson's? Writing recently in *The Gideon*, she had this to say:

"Although I was saved when twelve years old and brought up in a Christian home, the devil had me convinced that I couldn't talk to anybody about his or her soul's salvation. It was easy for me to pat myself on the back and to tell myself that I was doing more than anybody else in the church. But all this time I wasn't really satisfied or happy, for in those years I had never said a word to a single person about the Lord, or tried in any way to lead one to Him. I had always comforted myself with the thought that I could take them to church and let the preacher talk to them. That was the preacher's job anyway.

"Then one year as I was getting ready to take my four children to a young peoples' camp at Mt. Hermon, California, it occurred to me that I could take my husband's Sunday school class of boys with me. They were a pretty rough bunch, eight in all. Only two or three ever came to church, and only one was a Christian. Every one said I was crazy to tackle such a job. I got another woman to come and help me with the cooking. We rented a cabin in the tall redwood trees near Mt. Hermon and had a grand time. The boys were well behaved and I had no trouble at all. We attended the services every morning and evening.

"Every one had a grand time but me. I was miserable. The Lord was talking to my heart. I felt that I should talk to these boys about their souls, but I was afraid. I didn't know what to say or how to start. I argued that I was doing my part by bringing them there and taking them to church twice a day. I shouldn't have been worrying about it, but I didn't have any peace in my heart. Saturday night came, and not one of them had shown the least sign of wanting to be a Christian.

"The conference was closing on Sunday and I wanted to see them accept the Lord as their Saviour before we went home, but I didn't see how I could do anything about it. Isn't it too bad we have to come to the end of our rope and get desperate before we will let the Lord work through us? That night as I walked down the trail leading to our cabin, I was praying. Before I reached the cabin I promised the Lord that I would speak to the first boy I saw when I got home if He would give me the strength and words to say. I was so frightened, I could hardly climb the stairs, but I went ahead. As I stepped on the porch, two of the boys came around the cabin. I stopped them, but I was so frightened, I can't remember what I said to them. One of them said to me, 'I've been wishing you'd say something to me all week. I've been wanting to talk to you, but I didn't know how to start.' Just then two more boys came around the corner. The five of us sat on the porch and talked until late about the Lord. When I was alone in my room that night, I marveled at the freedom I had in talking to those boys and how easy it was to tell them the plan of salvation. Satan had made it seem so hard but when the first word was spoken, it wasn't hard at all.

"The next morning at the breakfast table all six of the boys accepted the Lord as their Saviour. What a day of rejoicing that was! The world talks about thrills, but there is no thrill in all the world that is comparable with the thrill of leading one soul to the Lord. Love will win them when everything else fails.

"And after I had finished, the leader of this missionary district group, a woman admired and loved by everyone, came to me with tears in her eyes and said, 'Mrs. LeTourneau, I don't know of a single person that I have ever led to the Lord.' What a tragedy! She was spending her time doing church work, organizing missionary groups, and many other very good and necessary works, but she had neglected the most important thing in life."

That the marriage of Robert LeTourneau and Evelyn Peterson was of the Lord the Christian fruitage of their lives together offers inspiring testimony. Neither Robert's wisdom, nor any human wisdom, could have found a woman more suited to the demands which were to be made upon her as his wife in the career lying ahead of him in the providence of God than Evelyn Peterson. It was true of Robert LeTourneau as it had been true of Adam when God said, "It is not good that the man should be alone; I will make him an help meet for him."

Robert's first business venture, when he started his career as a "land-leveling contractor," was the erec-

tion of the old Moss Avenue shop in Stockton. Here
he and Evelyn made their home and faced together
their first great sorrow—the loss of their first-born
child—a boy of four months. Other children came
during the years, six of them, one girl and five boys.
Between that first domestic sorrow and the most recent, twenty years went by. Then they lost their
second born, Donald, in the first flush of his young
manhood, leaving his bride of three months and his
father's hopes for his future gazing heavenward, *until
that day.*

The zest with which Evelyn LeTourneau assumed
her rôle as wife and helpmeet was not to be damp-
ened by personal sorrow or exhausted in domestic
duties. When her husband's business needed something in the way of help within the range of her
ability or strength, her response to the call was ade-
quate and unhesitating. More than once she took the
firm-and-family flivver, drove to the boat landing
some distance away, steering with one hand and holding on to her baby with the other, picked up a bar
or plate of rolled steel, or other material which was
needed at the plant in a hurry, and drove back with
it.

She made another important contribution to the
success of the business, more or less willingly, and
under the pressure of stern necessity. A rush order
for a scraper caught the shop without welding rods
and the proprietor without money to buy any.
Bronze was needed—at once. Whether Robert or

Evelyn thought first of the curtain rods over the windows in their home doesn't matter now. Down came the curtains and into the melting pot went the rods. Evelyn once said of this experience: "I really didn't mind curtainless windows, for I once worked in a laundry as a girl and ironed so many curtains that I vowed I'd never have curtains in my windows when I had my own home."

Her interest in her husband's business burned ever more and more brightly with the passing of the years. Fifteen years later, when the Peoria factory was established, Evelyn LeTourneau asked for permission to help in the task of unloading the first shipment of steel received at the plant and actually helped to unload the first carload by attaching her car to the rails and hauling some of them from freight car to truck.

During the first years of the family's residence in Peoria, the LeTourneau home was a sort of combined home and plant dormitory. So absorbingly interested is Mrs. LeTourneau in everything connected with her family and her husband's business, and in extending her Christian ministry to the young people who come within the circle of these interests, that she is unaware of any dividing line between family and workers or friends.

The author, who visited the LeTourneau home shortly after the family moved to Peoria, was surprised to find that in addition to the eight members of the family, about thirty young men, employed in the factory, were living in the same house and about on the same terms as other members of the family. In fact, one gained the impression that it was one big family of forty members. And besides that, there was at least one extra room for visitors, for I was taken in and lodged there with no apparent derangement or readjustment among the others. The dining room contained a long table with places for all, even a number of additional dinner guests. The spirit pervading the household was markedly Christian, evidenced by an absolute absence of bickering and confusion, and the presence everywhere of kindliness, consideration for the comfort of others, and joy in the Lord. Throughout all the details of material and spiritual ordering, the influence of that home's mother could be felt, leaving its impress most upon those who love its appearing, like "the ornament of a meek and quiet spirit, which is in the sight of God of great price."

Evelyn LeTourneau, like the wind that bloweth where it listeth, is not to be confined in one place or to a few interests. She is president and director of Bethany Camp for boys and girls, Winona Lake, Indiana, owned by the LeTourneau Foundation, where large numbers of boys and girls, under competent supervision, are given recreational privileges during the summer under conditions designed to improve health of body and soul. The work of Bethany Camp grows in importance year by year. The results which have been achieved there in converting boys and girls to lives of Christian service is a tribute to the devotion and ability of Mrs. Robert LeTourneau.

Mrs. LeTourneau took a lively interest in the weekend Gospel ministry which her husband inaugurated in churches and other Christian gatherings throughout the country some years ago. In the beginning and for several years, these trips were made by automobile, Mrs. LeTourneau often a member of the party, which also included a quartet of young men called "The King's Messengers."

One Monday morning in June, 1937, this little band of missionaries for Christ was driving along a Tennessee highway on their way to a meeting. Although they had been driving all night in order to be on time for their appointment, the driver, a member of the quartet, a careful and experienced man, was wide-awake and alert. The road was straight. It was broad daylight.

Coming toward them at a high rate of speed from the opposite direction was another car having three Negroes as occupants. Suddenly, when only a short distance from the LeTourneau car, the driver of the approaching car turned his head to talk to his companions in the rear seat. His car swerved sharply to the left. The two cars came together with a tremendous crash. A farmer from a near-by porch saw the whole thing.

Both cars were practically demolished and five persons killed outright. The dead were the three Negroes and two members of the LeTourneau quartet,

UPPER. Air view of hotel and auditorium and portion of Lake Louise, Toccoa, Ga.

CENTER. Hotel and auditorium, shortly after completion.

LOWER. Lake Louise, artificial lake created by damming stream, near Lake Louise Conference Grounds, Toccoa, Ga.

UPPER. First of the Louise Farming Co. buildings on 4,500 acre farm, at Toccoa, Ga., supplies LeTourneau community with dairy and other products.

LOWER. Portion of airport at Toccoa showing hangar, engine shop and school.

one being the driver. Four out of nine survived, one of them unhurt, the other three cruelly injured.

Mr. LeTourneau describes the accident in his own words:

"There was no excuse for it. Our driver took the shoulder of the road to our right, intending to give the other man the road and let him pass, but he shot clear over to our side, and we made a head-on collision. One of our party was unhurt. He dragged me out of the wreckage first. Both of my hips were driven out of their sockets, my pelvis was broken, a piece of bone was broken off the side of the hip socket, my chest was crushed, a leg was broken and a foot crushed. Strange to say, I did not lose consciousness. He dragged my wife out next. She was bruised and bleeding, cut from head to foot. I tried to talk to her but she was unconscious. Then the third living member of our party was pulled out, unconscious, and laid next to the others, his arm and collar-bone broken.

"I looked up to heaven and said, 'Lord, this could not have happened if You had not permitted it, because I know "that all things work together for good to them that love God." You suffered more than this for me. Thy will be done.'

"I said to our unhurt member, 'Bill, it looks like Evelyn and I are going. I don't care about the factories or the money, but promise me you will do your best to see that the children are brought up to know the Lord and serve Him.'

"God was so near that I wasn't anxious or worried. His presence was very real. I could say with Job, 'I have heard of Thee by the hearing of the ear: but now mine eye seeth Thee.' "

For the third or fourth time in his life, Robert LeTourneau was saved from physical death as by a miracle. Both he and his wife survived the accident, as did the third injured member of the party, and were restored to health, after weeks of severe suffering, with no souvenir of the accident left on his body save a slight limp. When the doctors saw Robert they told him he would never walk again. Four days after the accident, Mr. and Mrs. LeTourneau were back in their home in Peoria, having traveled 500 miles by ambulance. Robert was flat on his back for weeks but had himself pushed around the plant on his portable cot so that he was never out of touch with plant affairs during the time of his convalescence. He said recently:

"Lord, if sending such hardships is the only way to keep me in the place where I can know the fellowship of His sufferings, then help me to triumph with Him in bearing such afflictions.

"Today I stand as a living witness that the Lord Jesus Christ, Who intercedes for me at the right hand of God, is sufficient for body, soul, and spirit."

A year after R. G. LeTourneau and his wife were thus saved from physical death by the hand of God, an incident occurred that led the business into a still wider field of expansion than any hitherto known and Robert and Evelyn LeTourneau into fields of Christian ministry greater than anything they had ever dreamed of.

VIII

Georgia Adventure

"GOD MOVES in a mysterious way His wonders to perform," wrote William Cowper, the English poet. The circumstances which led Robert LeTourneau to build a factory in Toccoa, Georgia, may be traced to a seed dropped into the productive soil of his consciousness by the divine Husbandman through the human agency of one of His servants, Rev. R. A. Forrest, D. D., a Christian minister and also president of Toccoa Falls Institute, Toccoa Falls, Georgia, a tiny village situated three miles west of the town of Toccoa. Toccoa Falls Institute was founded by Dr. Forrest and his wife in 1911 to provide an educational institution in which the sons and daughters of the underprivileged mountain folk of that region might receive Christian and missionary training along vocational lines for service in the field.

In the year 1936 Dr. Forrest decided to celebrate the twenty-fifth anniversary of the founding of his school by making a trip around the world. He planned to visit former students of the Institute who had gone out as missionaries to foreign lands. On the way from Toccoa Falls to Seattle, Washington, from which port his steamer was to sail for Japan, Dr. Forrest stopped off at Omaha, Nebraska, to make an address before a convention being held there and present the work of his Institute. Another speaker before this same convention was Robert LeTourneau. They both came and made their speeches but did not meet.

After Dr. Forrest left Omaha, a friend of his, Dr. R. R. Brown, also a friend of Robert LeTourneau's, spoke to the latter about the excellent character of the work being done at Toccoa Falls Institute by Dr. Forrest. He had never heard of it. However, learning that Dr. Forrest was to speak in Hollywood, California, en route to Seattle, he tried to reach him there but missed him by a few hours. Arriving in Seattle, Dr. Forrest received a special delivery airmail letter with a check enclosed for $1000. Hearing that Dr. Forrest was to make a trip around the world, the writer of the letter said it had given him an idea, namely, that Dr. Forrest would probably find on his trip that many former students were having a tough time and that a little financial assistance might ease the going for them.

This generous gift was accepted by Dr. Forrest as from the hand of the Giver of every good and perfect gift. With unbounded gratitude to God for the thoughtfulness and generosity of one of His devoted servants, Dr. Forrest converted the check into travelers' checks of $10 and $20 denominations, and, in his own words, "left a swath of happiness around the world by gifts to humble folk who had no other way of getting help in time of need."

For every gift made by Dr. Forrest, a receipt was taken showing the reason for the gift and the purpose for which used. These receipts were sent to Mr. LeTourneau when Dr. Forrest returned from his trip, and the latter, much delighted with the way the money had been used and accounted for, invited Dr. Forrest to come and see him. Dr. Forrest did so and some time after his visit to Peoria he received a check for $10,000 for the work of the Toccoa Falls Institute, with a note saying that anyone who could be trusted with $1000 for use on the other side of the world could also be trusted with $10,000 for use on this side.

" 'Where your treasure is, there will your heart be also,' " quoted Dr. Forrest. "Since he made an investment, Mr. LeTourneau came to see us and appeared to be delighted with the Institute, the country, and the people. It cannot be said that any individual persuaded Mr. LeTourneau to build a factory in Georgia. He was definitely led of the Lord in this matter, I am certain. In less than a year after that visit a great factory was erected, hundreds of men were employed, and great machines were being manufactured. One of the first of the machines built in the Toccoa plant was purchased by the State of Georgia for use in a prison camp where first offenders and juveniles work on roads. The mechanical training these young prisoners receive enables many of them to earn an honest living after their terms expire."

On the human and business side, one of the reasons why R. G. LeTourneau decided to build a factory in Toccoa, Georgia, was that the manufacturing facilities of the Peoria factory were overtaxed. The decision to build at Toccoa was definitely made during the latter part of 1938, in line with the idea of decentralization of industry now being practiced by many of the larger industrial concerns.

In November, 1938, a small group of executives and workmen set out from Peoria to begin work on the construction of a new plant at Toccoa. A number of friends and a large audience of townspeople and country folk gathered on a plot of land two and a half miles from Toccoa for the groundbreaking ceremony. A band from the Toccoa High School furnished music. Robert LeTourneau pushed a shovel into the earth and turned over the first piece of sod on the site for the new factory. Then he and Mrs. LeTourneau climbed into a "Tournapull," then a new LeTourneau product, the latest addition to the line, and a demonstration was given of the uses to which the machine would be put in leveling the ground for the foundation of the new building. The building soon after erected measures 400 by 400 feet, 408 employees were engaged in erecting it, in building steel houses in which to live, and in making finished parts and equipment for the Peoria plant. Housing facilities in Toccoa were found to be inadequate for the accommodation of the company's employees so that a separate corporation had to be formed for the manufacture of products other than grading equipment. Twenty steel houses and several dormitories were fabricated and put up.

The new plant was dedicated on July 11, 1939. *The Atlanta Constitution*, a leading newspaper of the South, announced the event with a headline reading—

TOCCOA FACTORY IS DEDICATED TO PRINCIPLES OF CHRISTIANITY—GUIDANCE OF GOD IS IMPLORED FOR A $2,000,000 PLANT—BIG GATHERING OF FRIENDS AND EMPLOYEES CHEER DEDICATION OF POLICY IN REVIVAL-LIKE ATMOSPHERE

Part of the story printed by the newspaper follows:

"The strangest pact was recorded on a hilltop outside this North Georgian mountain city (Toccoa) when a multi-millionaire builder of road machinery dedicated his new factory to the guidance of God and His Son the Saviour of humanity.

"Between four and five thousand men, women and children leaped to their feet again and again to cheer while R. G. LeTourneau, America's foremost creator of road-building machinery, pleaded with them, his new-made friends, neighbors and employees, to join with him in helping God to solve the man-made problems of today's world by the simple means of honest work and brotherly love. They sat in startled bewilderment as they saw, for the first time, a type of American they had never seen before at close range—a successful captain of industry—confess how he had been won to the cause of Christianity. 'We need God,' he said. 'I know He is the only power that will solve our problems. The biggest step anyone can take is to give his heart to Jesus Christ. There is a sad condition in the world today. Multitudes are starving. We hear the argument of what we could accomplish if we had a man to show us what to do. We have that Man—that Man is my Saviour and your Saviour, the Lord Jesus Christ! If we would only listen to Him!'

"The large audience was packed row on row on wooden benches built on the concrete floor of the new plant. LeTourneau was convinced, he said, that a factory in that locality would bring him into contact with ambitious young Americans eager to earn their own living. Already more than two hundred North Georgians are working for him at this factory where prosperity has put all the citizens to work. On what was before merely a piece of woodland, a city of solid steel is to be built, populated by workmen enjoying wages rarely known in that section."

The dedication service was presided over by Rev. R. R. Brown, D.D., of Omaha, Nebraska, whose name was featured once before in this history—the man who first acquainted Mr. LeTourneau with the work of Dr. and Mrs. Forrest at Toccoa Falls Institute. Other speakers who addressed the dedication service that day were United States Senator Richard B. Russell; His Excellency, the Honorable E. D. Rivers, Governor of Georgia; Preston Arkwright, President of the Georgia Power Company; R. W. Wirt, Vice President of the Southern Railway System; Clyde McClure, City Attorney of Toccoa; W. J. Rothell, Chairman of the Stephens County Commission; and Jack Salvador, Superintendent of the new LeTourneau factory.

Telegrams of congratulation poured in by the score. One read:

"As you build machines to lift loads and remove mountains, may you realize your heart's desire in seeing burdens lifted from multitudes of weary, heavy-laden souls by the new birth, that blind eyes be opened, deaf ears unstopped, and the tongue of the dumb sing."

Stomach satisfaction for those attending the dedication service was provided by Mr. LeTourneau with the same thoroughness as he had offered soul satisfaction. A regulation "Southern Barbecue" was put on for which the head of the new factory furnished twenty hogs, thirty sheep, fourteen hundred pounds of beef, and thousands of bottles of soft drinks.

The feeding of five thousand on this occasion from the resources of one person who began his life's career with little save his talent and his faith in God, while not a miracle, did not fail to remind many of those who heard the story, of the lad who brought the little that he had—five barley loaves and two small fishes—just a small boy's lunch—and gave it to the Master for the feeding of a hungry multitude.

Every night for a week following the barbecue,

old-fashioned revival meetings were held. Hundreds accepted the Lord Jesus as their Saviour. Mr. Le-Tourneau could be seen at the close of the services, on his knees praying for the salvation of one or a number of persons, and for God's leading in the establishment of the new industry.

An item published in *The Toccoa Record* read:

"When Mr. LeTourneau decided to open a plant at Toccoa, he did our community its greatest favor. Not only does the plant turn a weekly pay roll of over $10,000 into our city, but the high moral standards of the LeTourneau personnel has added more than we can ever say to Toccoa's civic development."

An article in a North Carolina newspaper of July 27, 1939, wound up with the following paragraph:

"We, the Christian laymen of the South, welcome into our midst this man of God. He will be a challenge to every business man in this section of our land. What America needs so desperately is thousands of business men who will really consecrate themselves and their businesses to God. Peace and brotherly love would naturally follow and there would be no strife between capital and labor."

As to the success of the Toccoa project on its business side, figures for sales and earnings for the business as a whole, including the Toccoa operation, are as follows:

Year	Sales	Net Profits
1939	$ 7,731,325.16	$1,816,470.58
1940	10,740,845.51	1,858,228.58

From about 20 employees in 1929, the total number of people employed in Stockton, Peoria, and Toccoa by the end of 1940 was 2003.

The "Georgia Adventure" of Robert LeTourneau was of much practical value, as such undertakings are esteemed by the world, in the lives of a large number of people and to the community as anything he had ever done before. But it was also of far more spiritual value to those directly connected with the business and to a far larger number not connected directly with the business.

IX

Toccoa Benefits

ROBERT LeTOURNEAU'S interest in the work of the Toccoa Falls Institute continued after the building of his Toccoa factory. One of the early results of this interest was the decision on the part of Mr. and Mrs. LeTourneau to move their family and transfer their home from Peoria to Toccoa so that all of the children might profit by the Christian influences and educational advantages of the Institute. The oldest son, Donald, became a student while the family was still in Peoria. He had given his heart to Christ before coming to the Institute, and after coming found the surroundings and influences of the place conducive to the building up and strengthening of his Christian life. Shortly after the family settled in Toccoa, the second oldest LeTourneau boy entered the Institute as a student.

Mrs. LeTourneau's interest in Toccoa Falls Institute was as enthusiastic as her husband's. One of the first things she did to show the genuineness of her appreciation of the work of Dr. and Mrs. Forrest was as thoughtful as it was practical. The Forrests possessed an automobile of ancient vintage and uncertain performance which was their most-often used means of transportation and the source of much trouble to Dr. Forrest. Just before one of her visits to Toccoa, Mrs. LeTourneau purchased a new LaSalle and drove it from Indiana to the Institute. Upon arrival, she asked Dr. Forrest what he thought of her new car, and how he'd like to swap his for hers. With no thought of what she had in mind, he told her he'd have to have considerable to boot. She suggested he'd better try her car before trading. She got out and invited him to sit at the wheel. As soon as he did so, she quickly got into his old car and drove off, shouting, "Good-by!"

One very fine evidence of Mr. LeTourneau's deep interest in the work of Toccoa Falls Institute is a beautiful new building, recently opened, and containing a gymnasium, a large assembly hall, a dining room, and a girls' dormitory. This building, which cost over $40,000, is named "LeTourneau Hall," and is largely the gift of the man whose name it bears. It was constructed for the most part by the boys of the Institute. As an addition to the school plant it has enabled the Institute to accommodate a larger student body. Where before the new building was put into service, the enrollment was limited to 95 students, the number which can now be accommodated is 400. The proximity of the LeTourneau factory at Toccoa to the Institute, less than five miles, engenders advantages beneficial alike to the business, the school, and the youth of North Georgia and

North Carolina. Many of the young men attending the Institute are preparing for full-time Christian service and would have no other means of paying their way through school if there was not the opportunity to obtain employment which has been provided by the establishment of a factory so close at hand.

At the dedication of the new Institute building, senators, congressmen, and other outstanding political and Christian leaders, attended the services as a mark of honor to the Institute. Over the doorway of the new building are the words, "Where Character is Developed with Intellect."

Putting in an airport at Toccoa is another project to which Mr. LeTourneau has given much of his time and money. The building of this airport, one of the finest between Atlanta and Washington, D. C., has been greatly blest of God, as attested by the spiritual benefits which have already issued and which will continue to issue from it. Through an understanding which has been reached between LeTourneau and the United States Government, the National Youth Administration has agreed to invest funds in starting an aviation school in connection with Toccoa Falls Institute, on condition that he put up a large shop building and equip it for the training of students in aviation courses. In addition to this shop he has already built five dormitories, near the factory, each housing twenty-four students and an instructor. The school, it is clearly understood, is to be run in harmony with the Christian principles which prevail at Tococa Falls Institute.

The dormitories referred to are also a LeTourneau product. They are of all-steel construction, hermetically sealed and air-conditioned, with a six-inch insulated space between outside and inside walls, providing almost perfect protection against the heat of summer and the cold of winter. These houses are fire, earthquake, termite, and almost bomb proof. The walls both outside and inside are painted, and the general appearance is modern and attractive.

One of the local newspapers said of the airport:

"As he does so many things, R. G. LeTourneau lost little time in figuring how to construct an airport in our Georgia mountain country, where a hundred yards of flat ground is unusual. He merely picked out a small mountain, had his boys scrape off the top with one of their giant scrapers, and—presto!—came the airport! It has a 2000-yard four-direction runway, and a fine hangar. It is fully equipped with a beacon, landing field lights, and all other features.

"Many visitors at the LeTourneau plant, as they watch 'R. G.' go about the business, come to feel they are seeing a man who is developing a new 'Utopia' to show the entire nation how a Christian ideal can become a concrete fact."

Mr. R. W. Wirt, Vice President of the Southern Railway System, said on the occasion of the dedication of the Toccoa factory:

"It is a great pleasure and privilege for me, on be-

UPPER. A few of the 32 steel homes for employees on Pine Ridge, Toccoa.
LOWER. A closer view of one of the homes.

UPPER. The LeTourneau Empire in Georgia, comprising 5,500 acres, previously idle.

LOWER. Two years progress, LeTourneau plant and other buildings, employing 1,150 and still growing.

half of the Southern Railway System, to welcome this splendid new industry to Toccoa. What a blessing it is to this community that this intensely religious business man, who is our guest of honor, was, I sincerely believe, led by the Spirit to become acquainted with Dr. Forrest and learned of the great work he is doing at the Toccoa Falls Institute.

"The immediate results of the location of this new industry are now being seen on all sides. Think of the new money already put, and to be put, into circulation here by reason of the construction of this plant—new homes for workers, new stores, new service stations, and so on. Money spent in building always means more work and more business for all—labor, material dealers, and transportation companies —to name only a few.

"But the crowning purpose of the location of this industry here is that the Toccoa Falls Institute will provide a source from which to draw intelligent, well-educated young men for employment in this plant; and, more important, these young men can find employment here and will not be under the necessity of having to look for jobs elsewhere—perhaps in vain. Mr. LeTourneau, Sir, what a blessing to you that you have been enabled to provide a livelihood for hundreds of these young men and their dependents!

"People of this part of Georgia, and especially those in the mountain region, are nearly one hundred per cent native born. They are Americans of the type that has contributed more than any other factor to the wonderful industrial development in the territory served by the Southern Railway since its organization. Wage earners drawn from this great reservoir of native Americans, with generations of American ancestry behind them, are dependable and capable, and have shown their efficiency and adaptability in a wide variety of industries.

"The South has been termed the 'Nation's Number One Economic Problem.' But knowing the resources and opportunities of this territory, and the character of the people, we believe that the territory which our railway serves is the 'Nation's Number One Economic *Opportunity*.' "

That R. G. LeTourneau's business motives in locating his factory in the mountain country of Georgia were uninfluenced by any considerations other than the hopes born of his Christian faith is the testimony of Mr. Preston Arkwright, President of the Georgia Power Company, one of the biggest business enterprises in the State:

"There is no kinder philanthropy than the establishment of a useful business enterprise of this type. This man is not starting a sweatshop. He pays better wages than the average employer. He works his laborers reasonable hours. His employees need no protection. He came to our State with this magnificent industry of his own accord. No chamber of commerce inveigled him into building his plant in Georgia. Not a railroad ticket was spent to lure him into coming here. He received no land grant. He selected this property and bought it himself. He received no Reconstruction Finance Corporation loan. He received no PWA grant. All we see here today is individual enterprise. This is brand new wealth, adding to the wealth of our State. We were not charged a dollar to benefit from this added wealth. If it's a failure, you and I, the citizens of Georgia, don't lose a red cent. It's his risk. This man brings us the opportunity to earn our own way. This man gives these men from the mountains of North Georgia an opportunity to earn something worth while, to produce something useful. He will learn, as he gets to know the North Georgians better, that they will be one hundred per cent loyal to every one who treats them fairly. He will learn that these are the most generously responsive people in the world. I congratulate you on your new industry. We have had nothing like it in Georgia. Mr. LeTourneau, we want it to be profitable!"

On the occasion of the dedication of the Toccoa factory, one of the speakers was His Excellency, the Honorable E. D. Rivers, Governor of Georgia. The speech Mr. Rivers made on this occasion was widely quoted in the newspapers because of the reference it contained to the use Mr. LeTourneau had made of Christianity in his business, and the statement that such a use, if more widely practiced by other business men, would have a tendency to do away with the misunderstandings between capital and labor which result in strikes and the unrest produced by the teachings of Communism. Part of Mr. Rivers' speech was quoted in the newspapers as follows:

"Mr. LeTourneau had the means to go anywhere in the nation with his business. He would have been welcomed anywhere. But after looking the whole country over, he has come here to Georgia and the Southland. He is not going to find Communists and sitdown strikers in the South. (Loud cheering.) If we had more religious meetings like this in business, we wouldn't have so many strikes over the nation— neither would there be any development of 'Alien- ism.' (Louder cheering.) I think the greatest thing the country needs is the old-time religion and family altars in the home. I think that if we will go back to the old religious ways that the country will be better off. I firmly believe the business world of today needs a return to old-time religion. A spiritual revival is needed if America is to climb out of the present crisis."

The question is often asked of the head of the LeTourneau business, "Just how does Christianity work out actually, and what is the effect on your own people and your relations to the unions?"

No subject is of deeper interest to many people, Christian as well as non-Christian. The practical value of the teaching and practice of Christianity in changing the attitude of factory workers for the bet- ter and its usefulness in the amicable adjustment of labor differences is worth thinking about.

X

Christianity in the Shop

WHEN Robert LeTourneau built the 1937 addition to his Peoria factory he dedicated the plant to the service of God, as has already been described. A series of evangelistic services ran from Sunday to Friday. On that occasion a newspaper man took him aside and asked:

"I have to write this up but I don't just get the idea. What connection is there between this revival and building machinery? Do you feel it will build up the morale of your organization?"

Mr. LeTourneau answered: "Not only the morale but also the morals. We're trying to get men to believe in Jesus Christ, and better morale is only a by-product which is thrown in free."

Gospel meetings are usually held once a week in all LeTourneau plants. Attendance is voluntary. There is a meeting for the day shift at the lunch hour and another for the night shift at eleven o'clock. Mr. LeTourneau is a frequent speaker. On other occasions it is a visiting evangelist, or a factory employee. A quartet of workmen in overalls sing gospel hymns. The meetings are invariably crowded.

An idea spread that the way to get ahead in the LeTourneau business was to "be a Christian." Professing Christians, it was rumored, had the edge over those who were not Christians or who preferred not to make the claim openly, even when they were less efficient than non-Christian workers. Hearing of the humor, Mr. LeTourneau made it the subject of a talk to his factory people in which he said:

"I want it understood that while I believe a genuine Christian is apt to be a better workman than one who is not, we do not judge the work done by our workmen on this basis. There are plenty of people who claim to be Christians who haven't the real thing, and plenty of others who make no profession or claims and yet display more Christian graces than those who make the loudest claims.

"I make no apologies for the gospel meetings we hold in our plants. Their purpose is to promote the honor of our Lord Jesus Christ. Christianity is the essence of fair and square dealing. If there is anything done here in the name of Christianity which fails to give the same break to the man who does not profess to be a Christian as it gives to the man who does, then it is not Christainity. Don't you see that the minute you become partial or unfair, you violate the principles of Christianity?

"If you accept the Lord Jesus Christ as your Saviour, I feel you will make a better man and a better workman than if you do not have Jesus Christ in your heart. But you will never have that belief forced on you in this shop. Nobody is going to cram religion down your throat, because if they did, you'd throw it up about the second day. Unless you accept that belief of your own free will, nobody can make you believe it.

"We must have fair dealing here. I would be departing from the principles of Christianity if I favored one employee above another.. Every foreman in the shop who professes to be a Christian must act impartially.

"Word has come to me that this shop is made up of nothing but Christians. I only wish that were true. But if it were true, do you know what I would do? I'd bring in a lot of men who were not Christians, so we could give them the message of salvation and show them a living example of how to live Christ. It was reported to me the other day that a foreman saw two or three fellows idling during working hours and reproved them for it. One of them made the excuse, 'We're talking about the things of the Lord.' If they made that an excuse for loafing, it was no excuse. If you want to talk to a man about the Lord, say to him, 'Let's ride home together.' If he is an unbeliever and is fighting against God in his heart, such an invitation would disarm him more quickly than a sermon forced on him during working hours.

"I don't care who you are or where you come from, as long as you get your bread and butter here, you ought to be loyal to us. We would like to see you all loyal to Jesus Christ, but if you are not, we cannot demand it. If anyone is dismissed for disloyalty to the firm, he must not say that it was because he is not a Christian. Don't come to me when you are laid off and tell me that you have been treated unfairly because you are not a Christian. It will be your work, not your belief, that will be the deciding factor. Let Christ touch your life. He knows how. With His power within you, your service will become effective. You and I have only one life to live. We ought to make the most of it. 'Now is the accepted time; behold, now is the day of salvation!'"

Demonstrations of the power of the Gospel of Christ to change the hearts of men have not been lacking in the LeTourneau organization. A notable example occurred during a time of agitation among the men on account of certain efforts at unionization. As a result the employees formed an organization called the "LeTourneau Employees' Union." The man elected president was one who had been with the company for several years. He was liked by everybody, was a devoted Christian, loyal to his fellow men, and loyal to his employer—one of the self-sacrificing kind who would give the shirt off his back to any one in need. He served as president of the LeTourneau Employees' Union for a couple of years, then one day was taken sick and shortly thereafter died.

The vice president of the Union who then stepped into the presidency was about as different from the former president as it was possible for a man to be.

In plain language, he represented the saloon element. Christian members of the Union did much praying at this time, for all the signs pointed to trouble ahead and plenty of rough weather in the running of Union affairs.

A memorial service for the former president was held and an evangelist who had known and loved him was invited to conduct it. The service was held during the noon hour and a large gathering turned out. The new president, however, did not show up, probably because he was on the night shift, and also because in all probability he was not interested in spiritual things. Gospel meetings at the plants are always held twice, once at noon for the day shift and again at night for the night shift. The noon program is repeated at night, if possible. At the night meeting the new president was there but did not take charge. He sat with the others in the audience.

The evangelist gave a short message, and brought it to a close with an invitation to those present to indicate by the raised hand their desire to have prayer made for them. To the amazement of every one present, the new president raised his hand. And before the meeting broke up, he had given his heart to Jesus Christ. Of this incident, Mr. LeTourneau said:

"You can rest assured that that man did not make any trouble for anybody because of the change in his heart. He was a new creation in Christ Jesus, born again by the grace of God. He found a new teacher in the Lord. There was no worry after that among the Christian members of the Union as to whether they were going to get a square deal from that man."

During a series of Gospel meetings conducted by Evangelist Marion Reynolds in June, 1940, at the Peoria plant, a labor crisis occurred. The company's attempt to comply with the rules of the National Labor Relations Board caused the men to strike. Mr. LeTourneau asked Evangelist Reynolds to attempt a settlement. He settled the strike in one day. Confidence in the honesty of the man they work for, respect for his Christian beliefs by those who do not share them, and a high personal regard for him as a man and an employer, are among the factors which have reduced labor troubles at all LeTourneau factories to a minimum.

In another talk to his own people, Robert Le-Tourneau had something to say on Communism and un-American activities which has been widely quoted in the newspapers. The important point he never fails to make in all his addresses on this subject is the difference between Communism and Christianity and the value of the latter in every human and business relationship:

"Few people realize how much organized propaganda there is in America today. I believe in free speech, but I wish they would take every one that doesn't believe America is the finest land under the sun, that doesn't like our Government, that doesn't like our way of doing business, and wants to teach us a new social order, and pick up every one of them by the seat of the pants and set him on a boat bound for the land he does like.

"Communism is a doctrine of hatred. Christianity is a doctrine of love. They are as far apart as day is from night. Communism teaches us that we are not getting what is coming to us and we ought to fight for it. Christianity teaches us to love God and to love our fellow man and try to help him. I believe in that kind of practical Christianity."

On another occasion he said:

"I meet many folks who are seeking things that are not of the Kingdom of God. I get stacks of letters every day and thousands of people come to me seeking something for themselves. But so few come to me and say, 'I want to be saved—I want the Kingdom of God.' Nearly every one of them seeks something material. One man said, 'You know, Brother, we're told to come boldly.' I said, 'Yes, but you come to the wrong throne.'"

However, when the sincere seeker after the truth that is in Jesus Christ comes to R. G. LeTourneau, he finds one eager and ready to point the way.

XI

Personal Evangelism

R. G. LeTOURNEAU takes a personal interest in every one with whom he comes in contact and especially in those employed by the company who show the slightest interest in spiritual things. A man who had been with the company for a number of years came to him one day and said:

"I heard you say you'd be willing to talk to any of us at any time about the things of God."

"Yes—always."

"You have young men working here who seem to enjoy their Christianity. I've been trying to live a Christian life but I don't feel anything like what they talk about. Why is that?"

"Probably because you have never yielded your life to God in full surrender. Let's talk to the Lord about it," and they knelt in prayer—in the president's office.

He got up from his knees, a born-again believer, his face radiant with a new-found joy.

The next day, on his way to join a group who were holding a special prayer meeting on the bank of the river not far from the factory, Mr. LeTourneau saw this man kneeling in prayer under a tree by himself. When he later joined the meeting, he gave his testimony, telling the story of his recent conversion, and his joy in the Lord. He prayed that his fellow workmen in the factory might have the same joy in the saving power of Jesus' love which he had found.

There are men, like this one, who realize their need and take the initiative in seeking a remedy. There are others who stubbornly deny their need and avoid the help offered to them. Another employee of the company, a born mechanic and skilled workman, who had been with the firm for several years at the Peoria plant, was one of the class who seem to take special satisfaction in letting the world know that the moral standards of decent and law-abiding citizens mean nothing to them. This man was openly antagonistic to every form of Christianity. His influence upon his factory associates was demoralizing. He was discharged for drunkenness several times. Yet Mr. LeTourneau, determined not to be discouraged in his efforts at finding some way to put this man in the way of regeneration if possible, kept him on, and when after being discharged and out of work for long enough to become hard up, the man would apply for work again, he would take him back and give him another chance.

After the opening of the new factory at Toccoa, the idea occurred to Mr. LeTourneau that a fresh start in other surroundings and among new associates might be the means of arousing this man's better nature to a perception of what a new opportunity amidst the Christian surroundings and influence of the Toccoa Falls Institute might mean to him. He sent for him.

"I believe," he said when he had the man in his office, "that your only hope of keeping straight is to make a genuine surrender of your life to Jesus Christ. However, I can't force any man to become a Christian. But if you will promise me that you will attend church regularly and listen to the gospel messages, I'll give you a ticket to Toccoa and a job in the factory so that you can go down there and make a clean start. How about it?"

The man accepted the offer and went. It was just at the time of the dedication of the Toccoa plant. During the evangelistic meetings in the week that followed, the man was converted, and from that day to the present he has been a new creation in Christ Jesus from whom the old things are passed away.

People who do not believe in Christianity or the new birth, ascribe the claimed results of Christian believers to natural causes. A favorite explanation of the skeptic is, "It's just psychology, and the way you tell the story. A man reforms and the world says he turned over a new leaf; the Christian says he was born again. A man like Robert LeTourneau gives the credit for the results he achieves to his faith in God. But the world says it's merely personal ability and opportunity—in conjunction."

A man told Mr. LeTourneau that it was all very well for him to say that his success was the Lord's doing, but he—the man—didn't believe it. He said, "You just figured it out and figured it out right, and that is why you succeeded." To which he replied, "All right; but you'll have to give the Lord credit for giving me the brains to figure it out with."

A newspaper reporter who interviewed him printed the following description: "He's a big man, over six feet tall and more than two hundred pounds in weight. Except that his pockets are full of dough, he's a typical evangelist. When he witnesses for God at his meetings he waves his arms and shouts in a loud voice, 'My sins are gone, gone, gone! The more time I spend serving God, the more my business grows. Amen, Brother!' He lives on his salary, is anything but a snappy dresser, belongs to no country clubs, plays no golf. He has fits of temperament, but never swears, drinks or smokes."

Many of his business associates and the older men in the plants call him "Bob," and whether they agree with him or not, they find it neither helps them to agree or hurts them not to. His office—which visiting evangelists may use at any time—has in it a desk, and a couch, on which he sleeps when too busy to leave the plant at night. His bookshelves reveal his interests—the Bible, books on Christian missions and similar subjects, volumes on welding and aeronautics. On his desk is a sign which reads, "Jesus Never Fails," and a framed motto near it says, "Not how much of my money do I give to God, but how much of God's money do I keep for myself."

Robert LeTourneau's passion for winning souls to Jesus Christ derives its zest and joy from the memory of those sixteen years of unfruitfulness in the Lord which followed his conversion. For it was during those years that he had tried and failed so often to witness for his Lord—that caused him at last to cry, "Give me the backbone that I need and fill me with Your Spirit so that I can witness for You, and I'll do whatever You ask me from this day on." That God heard and answered this prayer needs no other proof than the record which he who runs may read, skeptic or unbeliever. He put himself and his human deficiencies in God's hands. He was a rough-neck to begin with, as he often says, and got his theology at mission meetings, and as for his education, it was knocked into him the hard way. "I attended a meeting in New York awhile ago," he said. "There was a gang there from the universities and they all had tags on them showing what college they belonged to. I had to have a tag so I wrote on mine, 'The School of Hard Knocks.'"

The Gordon College of Theology and Missions of Boston made him a director. A breakfast in his honor was held at the Parker House to which were invited a number of outstanding Christian leaders. Mr. Le-Tourneau was asked to speak and complied by telling the gathering how he was led into his week-end evangelistic ministry.

At the outset of his Christian experience, he said, he had no ability at all as a public speaker and always

UPPER. Steel dormitory accommodating 40 machinist apprentices, Toccoa.
LOWER. Radio station, WRLC, fully equipped, up-to-the-minute commercial radio station, LeTourneau owned, Toccoa.

UPPER. Gospel meeting in Peoria shop.
LOWER. Another shop meeting. Noon meetings are repeated at midnight for benefit of night shift.

stepped out in front of an audience with much diffi-
dence. However, he was very fond of young people
and often accompanied them when they conducted
the services at the downtown mission in Stockton.
He usually gave his personal testimony at these meetings and was always willing to talk with those who he
felt might be benefited by the inspiration he had
experienced in his own life. Those downtown mission
meetings, he said, were his seminary and the training
ground where he acquired whatever ability he possesses as a public speaker.

Later, he continued, his week-end campaigns of
speaking before Christian groups in far-away places
grew out of an incident which transpired after his
business was established at Peoria. Soon after the
opening of the factory there, the Peoria Association
of Commerce held its annual banquet. He attended
as a new member of the business community. Following the address of the principal speaker of the
evening, he was invited to tell the Association why
he had chosen Peoria as the location for his factory.
This opportunity appealed to him as an excellent one
for giving the influential citizens of Peoria his witness
as to God's leading in his business affairs. So he took
full advantage of it. The story he told that group that
night was probably a surprise that many of them were
wholly unprepared for. He told them first some of
the things they expected to hear about what a fine
city Peoria was and then he told them about his own
business and why it had become a success. His

business was a success, he said, because years before he came to Peoria he had made God his business partner. On that occasion he surrendered his business affairs to God's guidance, and God had blessed him and his business had prospered.

Naturally, such a speech by a successful business man attracted wide attention and caused a great deal of comment. As a result, he received several invitations to speak in the churches of Peoria, and in a short time he found himself spending his week-ends filling these speaking engagements. Soon calls began to come from churches and institutions outside Peoria, and, convinced that the Lord was leading him into a new and fruitful field of personal evangelism, he made this speaking ministry the subject of earnest prayer, and rejoiced to find the Lord kept opening new doors. Thus without giving up his business, or depriving it in any vital way of the benefits it derives from his inventive and managerial ability, he has become, without planning it that way in the beginning, a unique figure among Christian laymen. Instead of turning his business over to others to manage and devoting his full time to Christian service, he chooses, under God, to remain the head of his business and spend the time which other business executives generally give to recreation in telling as many people as possible about the Gospel of the Son of God and its power to save sinful men.

The LeTourneau business was established in Peoria in 1935 and from then until the fatal automobile accident of June, 1937, when five persons lost their lives, and Mr. and Mrs. LeTourneau, with two members of their quartet, were saved by God's miraculous intervention, as he truly believes, trips to and from the week-end meetings were generally made by car. Not long after their physical restoration, two considerations led them to seek a better mode of transportation than the automobile—the opportunity of attending a larger number of meetings by making better time in traveling and the ability to get to the far-away places. First, one airplane was purchased as an improved means of transportation over the car, and now five are in service for these week-end Gospel excursions. Mr. LeTourneau travels an average of 4000 miles a week and last year flew more than 200,000 miles—not to sell earth-leveling machinery, as someone has said, but to preach the Gospel. Still, he generally carries a portable drafting board with him on his flying trips with the help of which he sketches designs for equipment and machines while several thousand feet up in the air. Not much has been said in this narrative about Robert LeTourneau's accomplishments as an inventor. This may be the proper place to record the fact—since many people have wondered when he finds the time—that he has to his credit about fifty basic patents which have played their part in the successful operation of his plants and their products.

Two of Mr. LeTourneau's planes are transport ships, large enough to accommodate himself and

Mrs. LeTourneau or Dr. Harold Strathearn, Mrs. Dorothy M. Strathearn, known as "The Gospel Nightingale," whose beautiful soprano voice has thrilled thousands; and at other times, a quartet of singing workers from the factory, a couple of violinists, or a group of Negro singers called "The Carolina Gospel Quartet." Sometimes a plane will be used to carry the basketball team from Peoria to Toccoa, or vice versa. LeTourneau's speaking engagements are booked ahead for two years. If he were to comply with all the requests received, he would have to speak three times a day throughout that period. As it is, he often works sixteen hours a day, uses a gasoline scooter to get around his plants, and sleeps on the couch in his office instead of going home to go to bed.

A typical week-end schedule of speaking engagements is:

Huntington, W. Va.
>   Saturday,
>> 7:45 p. m.—Huntington City Mission.
>> 6:00 p. m.—Business Men's Banquet.
>   Sunday,
>> 10:45 a. m.—Fifth Avenue Baptist Church.
>> 2:30 p. m.—Union Service, City Auditorium.
>> 7:30 p. m.—First Methodist Church.

Chattanooga, Tenn.
>   Monday,
>> 6:00 p. m.—Second Presbyterian Church.

Chicago, Ill.

Tuesday,

    8:00 p. m.—Moody Bible Institute, Founder's Week Conference.

Corpus Christi, Texas.

Sunday,

    10:00 a. m.—Central Baptist Church.

    11:00 a. m.—First Baptist Church.

    3:00 p. m.—First Presbyterian Church.

    7:30 p. m.—First Baptist Church.

To get to Huntington, West Virginia, in time for the Business Men's Banquet at six o'clock on Saturday evening, he would fly from Peoria on Saturday afternoon, stay in Huntington over Sunday, and go on to Toccoa after the service Sunday evening. This would enable him to work at the plant almost the whole day Monday, flying over to Chattanooga in time for the six o'clock meeting that evening. Tuesday morning he would be in Peoria and after working the day, reach Chicago for the eight o'clock meeting that night at the Moody Bible Institute.

That traveling by plane is not without its thrills and uncertainties—on the human side—the following introduction to one of LeTourneau's talks will illustrate:

"I am glad to be here all in one piece. I suppose you all heard about how we got hung up in the sky the other day and could not get down. Everything came out all right, but it was a funny feeling circling around for two hours watching the folks down on the landing field as they gathered the doctors, the ambulances, and the fire wagons, and about two hundred spectators, while we waited for our gasoline supply to run out. We reached Toccoa about eight o'clock in the morning. When we tried to let down the landing wheels and found they wouldn't go down, we decided that we just wouldn't say anything to the folks below, and fly to Anderson, South Carolina, where the field is wider. But the folks at Toccoa were too smart for us. They saw us circling the port, and then sail off. So they tuned their radios in on our frequency and heard us telling Anderson about our predicament. Then a bunch of them jumped into their cars and came over to meet us. We appreciated the spirit of concern for our welfare shown by every one. When we finally landed, we came down as smooth as anybody could wish. Well, it broke the monotony in Toccoa for a few hours anyway."

In 1935, shortly after the LeTourneau family moved to Peoria, the author visited the home. When the family moved to Toccoa in 1939, he was invited to visit them there. The circumstances under which this visit was made bore a striking contrast to the circumstances surrounding the Peoria visit. I will attempt to describe them.

Mr. LeTourneau was speaking on Saturday in Bridgeport, Connecticut. He had spoken six times to six different audiences that day, including a mass meeting in the largest auditorium in town. I was invited to accompany him back to Toccoa in his twin-motored Lockheed plane—a nine-hundred-mile flight by night.

As we glided skyward the innumerable lights of the city below us seemed to be a reflection of the stars above. Automobile headlights looked like tiny fireflies going in all directions. Lighted railway trains seemed like Christmas toys. We passed, in a few minutes, over New York, sighting Rockefeller Center, the Empire State Building, the Statue of Liberty. As we passed Washington, we saw the Lincoln Memorial and the Washington Monument.

Four and a half hours of flight brought us to Toccoa, Georgia, after stopping at Washington, D. C., and Greensboro, North Carolina. It was an experience never to be forgotten because one of the wonders of the age in which we live. Shortly after landing at the airport in Toccoa we reached the Le-Tourneau home, still not too late for a good night's rest.

On the morrow it was my privilege to observe several new aspects of the Toccoa work not only in the way of Christian benefits but also much that was interesting and significant in the way of social and civic improvement.

XII

Of Farms and Conferences

BUILDING a factory in the mountain country of North Georgia does not mean what building a factory would mean near a large city like Chicago, or even Peoria, where there is an already established community. Toccoa has about five thousand population. Stephens County, which includes Toccoa, the village of Toccoa Falls, three miles away, and numerous other towns and villages, has a total population of only twelve thousand. So that building the LeTourneau plant two and a half miles from Toccoa meant establishing a community to go with it. The factory is east of Toccoa, the Institute west of it.

About four hundred employees were engaged in building the factory. They had to be housed, not in Toccoa, but in the immediate vicinity of the plant, with food and other necessities within reach. One of the immediate needs was good milk for the children and mothers. Milk in that region was scarce and not of the best quality. Mr. LeTourneau organized a new company, called the Louise Farming Company, Inc., having a capital of $15,000, and named after his only daughter, Louise LeTourneau, formerly an office worker in the Toccoa factory and now married to a young man employed in the plant. The purpose of the company is to give employees low cost housing, transportation and food. The interests of the company include a 4500-acre farm, stocked with registered cattle and farm animals, a dairy, a bus line between Toccoa and the factory, and a small canning factory. For the housing of employees, the "Tournapull Housing Corporation" was organized in 1941. The erection and renting of LeTourneau steel houses to employees is carried on at cost.

This farming enterprise is as efficiently managed as all the other LeTourneau projects. The purpose underlying its operation is the supplying of milk and other food to the families of employees at the lowest possible prices and not to see how much money can be made. Visitors to Toccoa are always interested in visiting the farm and asking questions about how the farm is operated. However, the farm is only one of many original features connected with the Toccoa adventure which were wholly unforeseen when it was first proposed to build a factory there.

By far the most spectacular development at Toccoa is the "Hotel and Auditorium" which forms the central feature of the "Lake Louise Conference Grounds," again named after Mr. LeTourneau's daughter. This beautiful building, constructed from plans designed by Mrs. LeTourneau, was erected primarily to meet the needs of the Christian Business Men's Committee International, a world-wide organization of which Mr. LeTourneau was recently elected president. When the building was completed, he invited the committee to hold its meetings in Toccoa. This great all-steel structure consists of a dome-shaped auditorium at the center, one hundred and twenty feet in diameter, with seating capacity for 1,686 persons, and is made without central supports. The hotel office and bookstand are also located in this section. From the circumference of this circular auditorium radiate seven wings, like the spokes of a wheel, each 110 feet long by 32 feet wide, in which are rooms for guests ranging from those with private bath to dormitories accommodating twenty-two persons. One of the wings houses a modern kitchen, and a dining room in which two hundred people can be seated and served at one time.

Lake Louise Conference Grounds, with its beautiful hotel and auditorium building, is offered as a meeting place for evangelical Christian gatherings and organizations. That Toccoa may become a great center from which the light of the Gospel of Salvation may stream to the far places of the earth is the hope of its founders, Robert and Evelyn LeTourneau. To make the conference grounds still more attractive, Mr. LeTourneau, skilful in the building of dams, saw where he could create an artificial lake with a shore line of twenty-five miles and a depth in many places of seventy-five feet by throwing a fifteen-hundred-foot dam across the lower end of the large stream which ran conveniently near the property. The dam was built, the lake came into being and was promptly named "Lake Louise," and boating, canoeing, fishing, swimming, surf-board riding, and other water sports, are at the pleasure, in season, of those attending conferences. Mr. LeTourneau himself is fond of every kind of water sport and is an ardent patron of the facilities offered at Lake Louise during the summer.

The development of Lake Louise Conference Grounds at Toccoa has an intimate relationship with the Christian welfare of employees at the LeTourneau factory and a strong but less direct relationship with the work of Toccoa Falls Institute. Along with this interest in the workman's and student's Christian welfare there is a corresponding interest in his mental, vocational, and industrial welfare. One thing Mr. LeTourneau aims at in all his plants is year-round employment, even though demand for the company's products is seasonal. This consideration receives special attention at Toccoa because of the necessity of providing work for Institute students who must pay their own way, or most of it.

The policy of the company is to encourage employees to advance themselves and seek positions of more and more responsibility and higher compensation in the company. Merit, loyalty, and ambition are therefore recognized and rewarded. To help them fit themselves for doing their work more efficiently and become eligible for advancement, a program of vocational and industrial training was inaugurated in 1938 and has been continued.

This educational program started with a home-study course in elementary mathematics. By the end of 1940 over fifteen hundred certificates had been issued for completed courses in leadership, mathematics, blue-print reading, welding, and machine-tool operation.

Early in the summer of 1941 the Peoria school was greatly expanded. Lectures and class study replaced the home-study program. Initial courses offered included shop mathematics, blue-print reading, machine-tool operation, flame cutting, and arc welding and welding symbols. Additional subjects are added when requested by ten or more workers. Foremen and specialized workmen provide trained, experienced instructors. All courses are open to the general public. Each subject requires student attendance two nights a week for three hours. All work is done in classroom periods. No outside study is expected. Courses are completed in ten weeks.

This educational program is organized under the Defense Education Act at the request of the Peoria Advisory Committee for National Defense Education, and in accordance with the LeTourneau company's policy of giving its employees the best opportunity possible for study and self-improvement.

The educational program being followed at the Toccoa plant has already been approved by the Georgia Department of Industrial Vocational Education and the County Board of Education. Certificates recognized throughout the State are offered. Class work and thoroughly organized courses are available in a wide variety of subjects, from elementary mathematics, to physics, chemistry, metallurgy, business law, marketing, and electricity.

R. G. LeTourneau's career has been a living demonstration of one of his favorite Scripture texts, namely, "Seek ye first the kingdom of God, and his righteousness; and all these things shall be added unto you." Speaking on this text to audiences in all parts of the country, he never fails to acknowledge his gratitude to God for the success of his business and to show that God has never permitted him, His servant, to outgive Him. Exactly how God has prospered him since he made God his business partner, and how much of this wealth he has given away to others, is brought out strikingly in a radio interview arranged between Robert LeTourneau and Robert Ripley.

Ripley, of "Believe-it-or-not" fame, invited Mr. LeTourneau to appear on his radio broadcast of September 27, 1940, and among the many interesting questions Mr. Ripley asked and Mr. LeTourneau answered were the following:

RIPLEY: Tell us what happened after you made God your partner.

LeTOURNEAU: The minute I started that partnership, business boomed. The next year my sales were over $100,000. The second year over $150,000. The third year over $200,000. Then we hit almost $400,-

ooo. It kept going like that, in leaps and bounds. In 1939 our sales were over $7,000,000.

RIPLEY: All because of your partnership with God! What was God's share in your business?

LETOURNEAU: I set aside 90 per cent of the stock for God's use.

RIPLEY: Then actually 90 per cent of your personal wealth goes to Christian activity? I understand that in the last year $1,200,000 of your profits went to God's work.

LETOURNEAU: Yes. To date more than $10,000,000 has been God's share.

RIPLEY: Then you keep very little money for yourself?

LETOURNEAU: Yes. You see, I don't feel that my brain made this money. I believe that the Lord made it possible for me to make it, and I'm only returning to God what belongs to Him. My motto is: "Not how much of my money do I give to God, but how much of God's money do I keep for myself."

RIPLEY: What do you do with God's share of the money?

LETOURNEAU: I established a foundation which supports a number of foreign missions and employs twelve evangelists, who travel over the country and speak in churches. We send out 1,500,000 pamphlets every month. And we have a publication called NOW which is mailed, free for the asking, to 80,000 people weekly. (NOW has since grown to 175,000 circulation weekly.)

RIPLEY: And of such is the working of Faith.

LeTOURNEAU: My philosophy is very simple, Mr. Ripley. There are two things I like to do. One is to design machinery, turn on the power, and see it work. The other is to tell people about the power of the Gospel and see it work in their lives. Jesus was willing to become poor, that we, through His poverty, might become rich. So, for any success I have had, I humbly thank God.

RIPLEY: In conclusion, I can think of nothing more appropriate to say than to quote to you from the greatest sermon ever given, "Let your light so shine before men, that they may see your good works, and glorify your Father who is in heaven."

The questions and answers which have been quoted in the foregoing interview are quoted from a leaflet which Mr. LeTourneau published by special permission of Robert Ripley and Believe It Or Not, Inc. The broadcast was nation-wide through the facilities of the Columbia Broadcasting System. As a result of the broadcast, many people have wanted to know more of the "Foundation" which Mr. LeTourneau referred to in his interview with Mr. Ripley.

XIII

The Lord's Treasury

COMPLETE absorption in the task at hand, it was recorded on an earlier page of this journal, is one of Robert LeTourneau's characteristics. As a boy he loved to play checkers—and win. Once, after a companion had beaten him, he lay awake all night planning how at their next meeting he might be able to outmaneuver him and come off victorious. At another time, with equal ardor, he loved to play "Give Away," the object of the game being not to win but to lose, and he probably derived as much satisfaction from one as from the other, judging by the pleasure he derives now from winning at the larger game of "Give Away," which he has since learned to play with God as his partner. But when he tries to outgive the Lord, he says, he loses every time; for he receives from God far more than he is able to give away.

In 1935 Mr. LeTourneau organized what he called "The Lord's Treasury." Its official title is "The LeTourneau Foundation." R. G. LeTourneau, Inc., is a California corporation, the corporate office of which is in Stockton, California, and the executive office of which is in Peoria, Illinois. A subsidiary is

UPPER. Dedication of new offices, Peoria; speaker—R. G.
LOWER. Two action shots of R. G.

UPPER. R. G. LeTourneau and Pilot Bill Retts, with new Waco, 5-place plane.
LOWER. R. G. (left) with party and Lockheed 7-passenger plane.

the LeTourneau Company of Georgia. The Louise Farming Company, Inc., is a Georgia corporation, the shares of which are owned by the LeTourneau Company of Georgia. On October 14, 1939, under an option agreement made late in 1938, R. G. LeTourneau, Inc., took over the entire investment of the Georgia company from The LeTourneau Foundation at cost, making the LeTourneau Company of Georgia a wholly-owned subsidiary of R. G. LeTourneau, Inc.

Of the 450,000 shares of issued capital stock of R. G. LeTourneau, Inc., 317,641 shares are held by The LeTourneau Foundation. The other 132,359 shares are held as follows:

Number of Shares Held	Number of Shareholders	Total Shares Held
1-50	760	19,510
51-99	44	3,092
100-200	374	48,216
201-300	33	8,905
301-400	16	6,065
401-500	11	5,395
501-1,000	19	13,845
1,001-10,000	9	27,331
	1,266	132,359
The LeTourneau Foundation	1	317,641
	1,267	450,000

Earnings per share for 1940 were $4.13 as compared with $4.03 for 1939 and $3.13 for 1938. The profit dollar is divided 24 cents for dividends, 40 cents for increased manufacturing facilities, and 36 cents for increased miscellaneous and working capital. LeTourneau common is currently quoted on the New York Curb, 28 bid, 30½ asked; preferred over-counter 101 bid, 102 asked.

The company increased its manufacturing facilities during 1940 through the expenditure of $1,104,000 for machinery, equipment, and plant expansion. Approximately 110,828 square feet of floor space were added in Georgia and 94,920 square feet of floor space were added at the Peoria plant.

The LeTourneau Foundation, which is the twelfth largest in this country, and the largest religious foundation, has a net worth of over $13,000,000. The Foundation increased its holdings during the year 1940 from 303,800 shares to 317,641 shares, which is equal to 70.6 per cent of the 450,000 shares issued and outstanding. It is a non-sectarian membership corporation organized "To teach, promulgate and disseminate the Gospel of Jesus Christ throughout the world, and also to unite in Christian fellowship the large number of consecrated Christians in the various evangelical churches, and for such purpose, to appoint and engage ministers, evangelists, missionaries, and others, to actively pursue and accomplish the foregoing purposes."

The gifts The Foundation dispenses are made possible from the dividends it receives as a stockholder of R. G. LeTourneau, Inc. In view of Mr. LeTourneau setting up The Foundation with 99 per cent of his personal wealth, it is interesting to note that he now owns only one thousand shares of LeTourneau stock. Before he gave the bulk of it to The Foundation and made the rest available for purchase, he owned it all.

Actual contributions made to outside organizations by The Foundation from the time of its inception in 1935, total $1,067,000. Substantial gifts have been made to Bible-believing schools, faith missions carrying on an evangelical program, and to deserving, faith-believing persons. These contributions are in addition to the activities carried on directly by The Foundation, such as tracts, publication and distribution of NOW, Bethany Camp of Winona Lake, Lake Louise Camp, of Toccoa, and the LeTourneau Christian Camp, Canandaigua, New York.

The LeTourneau Evangelistic Center, Suite 607, Rockefeller Center, 1270 Sixth Avenue, New York City, co-ordinates the work of The LeTourneau Foundation and its many interests. A fuller description of these interests and activities forms the concluding chapter of this history.

In the matter of giving, R. G. LeTourneau considers himself merely a steward of the money God has placed at his disposal. His oft-repeated statement is that he gives away 90 per cent of his earnings to the Lord's work and that to date this adds up to

$12,000,000. He contributes large gifts to Christian causes wherever he is assured they are worthy. His missionary interests are far-reaching, in fact, world-wide. Many colleges and schools have been saved from the sheriff's hammer as the result of Mr. Le-Tourneau's vision and generosity. The cost of his time and the expenses of his week-end evangelistic trips by aeroplane are borne by The LeTourneau Foundation and are therefore wholly without cost to the churches and institutions he visits.

Disseminating the Gospel by means of the printed word is also one of the important activities of The LeTourneau Foundation. Nearly three million tracts a month are distributed through the LeTourneau Evangelistic Center, in addition to the weekly pamphlet *NOW*.

Presidents of large corporations follow the custom of making an annual report to their stockholders and circulating this report in printed form so that all who own stock in the corporation may see for themselves what their officers and directors have been doing with the business in which the stockholder has an interest. One of the strangest documents ever to be presented by a corporation president to his stockholders was the annual report which R. G. LeTourneau handed to his stockholders for the year ending December 31, 1939. It was entitled, "A Decade of Progress from 1929 to 1939." Not many commercial corporations organized for profit have presidents who address their stockholders as Mr. LeTourneau did. His personal message introducing the report read as follows:

"I am trying to keep my eyes on a star and my feet on the ground. I am sorry for those who are so materialistic that they can't see God. On the other hand, I have little patience for those who expect the Lord to bring them everything they ask for on a silver platter. If we love the Lord, we will work for Him.

"In view of this, my week-ends are occupied in flying to all parts of the country giving the Gospel message to many different denominations and creeds. As a result, many definite cases can be pointed out where those contacted through the week-end visits, as well as those in our shops who hear the message, have had their lives transformed and lifted to a higher plane, with a resultant higher efficiency and loyalty.

"Someone has said, 'If a workman continues his work steadily and faithfully eight hours a day and doesn't worry, some day he will get to be the boss and then he can work sixteen hours a day and have all the worry.' I can work sixteen hours a day, but I do a minimum amount of worry, because I am endeavoring to accomplish what I believe God wants me to do and this eliminates any necessity for worry.

"Just as in the redesigning of a machine that is giving trouble, I try to analyze the cause of the strain and get at the root of the trouble which may develop in some other part of the machine. So in studying our Christian life I am confident that the root of the trouble is our heart attitude toward God. If our heart is right toward Him and we fit into His program, we can depend upon Him when the problems get beyond our control."

Only those who know the man who wrote these words are able to appreciate the depth of his sincerity and the reality of his faith. Long before there was enough to the business to warrant incorporation—back in 1920, when the harvests of the present LeTourneau business were seeds just being planted—God had been definitely and decisively taken into partnership. Is it any wonder that the divine Partner is mentioned by name and at length in the president's introduction to his annual report to stockholders?

Equally interesting is the "President's Personal Message" in his 1940 annual report:

"The law of 'survival of the fittest' is a hard, cruel law. We don't like it, but it is one of nature's laws we have to deal with. That's why this nation is traveling full speed ahead in a preparedness program. Our factories are co-operating with our Government in assisting to solve many of the mechanical problems, and the Georgia plant has contracted to do about six million dollars' worth of machining on forgings which will be produced at the Birmingham steel mills.

"I believe in preparedness, but it seems a shame to spend so much time and energy on instruments of destruction when we should be making useful instruments of construction. It only goes to show that the world needs a manager—one who would be smart enough, fair enough, good enough, and have confidence enough placed in him, so that he could handle the situation with complete control. The only one capable of handling this job is my Saviour, the Lord Jesus Christ. I have asked Him to become my manager.

"In making this report to a world that is bleeding and torn with hatred, strife, and selfishness, it might be well to remember that spiritual things are worth more than material things. Jesus said, 'Lay up for yourselves treasures in heaven.'

"I love Him because He suffered for me, and I am trying to serve Him, not just so He will take me to heaven when I die, but because I have caught a vision of His marvelous program, and I want to take part in that Program both here and hereafter."

What sort of a business is this business of LeTourneau's anyway? Is it important in an economic sense? Does it contribute to national as well as local well-being? About three thousand people are employed at the three plants, and many others are directly and indirectly benefited in a financial way. But how do the manufactured products of the concern help in lightening human labor and improving the material conditions of our social and industrial life?

One way to answer these questions is to name the machines manufactured by R. G. LeTourneau, Inc. But land-leveling machines—scrapers, haulers, excavators, rooters, tractor-cranes, rollers—are not interesting for what they are so much as for what they can do. Therefore, in what way have the use of these machines added to the country's industrial wealth?

Few people realize the long list of different kinds of private and public works going on all the time— everywhere—in connection with which dirt—enormous quantities of it—has to be moved from one place to another with great speed. Highways, dams, railroads, playgrounds, reservoirs, housing and factory sites, airports, levees and sea walls, are the kinds of projects referred to. Moving dirt was formerly accomplished by hand, and still is in many places on smaller projects. Groups of men with shovels fill a wagon, then wait for it to pull out while another pulls in. And so on for days and weeks. Today dirt is hauled by tractor-drawn machines. The use of machines in place of hand labor has created jobs for vast throngs of men by accelerating the whole program of public works construction throughout the entire world. Motor transportation demands more and better highways all the time—to mention one class of project only—and the way these projects are multiplying in number is giving employment to thousands in every locality where, before machines were used, only a few men could be employed. Providing ways to haul more dirt in less time is the job for which—in the hard language of business—LeTourneau products are manufactured. When they fail to drag more cubic yards of dirt faster and at less cost than machines of competitive make, then the business now being run by R. G. LeTourneau won't be so profitable as it is now. However, the man now running the business seems to have resources which have been very effective up to the present. Not only are improvements being made in present machines, but new types of machines are being added to the line from time to time. Not only does the company continue to sell its products to contractors and governmental agencies for use on highway, dam, airport, and similar projects, for which such products were originally designed and which projects still constitute the bulk of the work done, but new uses for LeTourneau machines are coming along all the time, such as sales to logging companies for cutting logging roads through the woods, to mines for removing overburden material, and for use in pits and quarries, oil fields, brick and clay plants, power plants, coal pits, and military establishments.

The business is twenty-one years old, as these words are written. From 1920 to 1929 it learned to take nourishment and exercise, and gather experience. Then it was incorporated. From 1930 to 1940 it grew from sales of $110,808.60 to $10,740,845.51. The sales and distributing organization in the United States consists of about two hundred agencies, and about two hundred in foreign countries up to the start of World War No. 2. Of the total sales, 5.2 per cent were made directly to the United States Government; 23.8 per cent went into foreign territory; 71 per cent were domestic. Some of the more notable projects for which LeTourneau machines were used in this country are the Golden Gate Bridge (north approach) San Francisco; Boulder Dam, Grand Coulee Dam, Trans-Florida Ship Canal, All-American Canal, the Pennsylvania Turnpike, America's finest military road; the Des Moines Airport, and innumerable others. England used LeTourneau equipment in building all types of public works—reservoirs (the famous Chingford Reservoir), playgrounds, sea walls, housing projects, airports, and in recent defense preparations. Canada is using scores of LeTourneau machines in its gigantic air-training program. France, before the German conquest, built fourteen airports using LeTourneau machines. They have been and still are used extensively for similar work in Mexico, Brazil, Argentina, Trinidad, Belgium, Russia, Italy, Iraq (the Kut Barrage), Cape Province, Dutch East Indies, Kenya Colony, Singapore, Malaya, Cuba, and the Hawaiian Islands. Altogether Mr. LeTourneau's machines have been purchased for use in eighty-six foreign countries. Sales to foreign countries for 1940 increased 10.8 per cent over 1939—42 per cent of the increase being sales to France and England.

To supply the demand for LeTourneau products in Australia, New Zealand, Dutch East Indies, and India, a new factory, 50 by 150 feet, known as R. G. LeTourneau (Aust.) Pty., Ltd., was erected fifteen miles from Sydney, Australia, in the summer of 1941. Seventy-five per cent of the cost was financed by R. G.

LeTourneau, Inc., and twenty-five per cent by C. E. Bryant, an Australian engineer.

The line of products is described as "The World's Most Complete Line of Modern Tractor-Drawn Earthmoving Equipment." Calling them by their trade names, they are "Tournapulls," in four sizes; "Angledozers" and "Bulldozers," for all size tractors; "Carryall Scrapers," in a range of sizes; "Tournatrailers," in a range of sizes; "Rooters," in three sizes and various depths; "Tractor Cranes" and "Tournacranes," in three boom lengths; "Sheep's Foot Rollers," in two sizes; and "Power Control Units," for operating all LeTourneau mechanical tools, available in single, double, and four-drum units.

Some people, when informed that selling prices for LeTourneau machines range from $300 for a single-drum Power Control Unit to $9,840 for a Model W, Single Bucket, Carryall Scraper with Model T Double Drum Power Control Unit, wonder where the saving comes in for those who have to buy them, especially when several sizes and varieties need to be purchased for a single project. The saving comes in, in reducing labor and time and in lowering the cost of the work to the taxpayers. In former days the high cost of human labor made public works on a large scale almost prohibitive. The need for better highways, dams, playgrounds, and other modern developments, made it imperative to find cost-reducing ways to build them.

Visitors to the factories at Peoria and Toccoa invariably want to make a trip through the plant. Believing that the reader is not contemplating an early visit either to Peoria or Toccoa, and yet would like to get some idea of what these factories look like on the inside—and what the men who work in them look like on the outside—an armchair journey through the Peoria plant will now be made.

XIV

Trip Through the Plant

SOME time after the Peoria factory had been built, a couple of students from the Bible Institute of Los Angeles (Biola), having heard of R. G. LeTourneau's work, decided they would like to see it for themselves. While on a trip east they made their plans accordingly and arrived in Peoria one morning. They telephoned the LeTourneau factory office about eight o'clock and were informed that Mr. LeTourneau was in the plant, had been there since about seven, and would probably be there until nine or ten that evening unless he had a speaking engagement to take him away. Did they wish to talk with him on the telephone, or would they call?

They decided to call. The plant is on the outskirts of town and is by no means easy for a stranger to find on his first visit. In those early days—the factory had been built about a year—calling at the plant was like a descent into Mudhaven, especially in late spring or during a wet week. Sidewalks have since changed all this. But the two Biola students could not have been discouraged if the LeTourneau factory had been located in the center of Dismal Swamp.

They arrived and asked to see Mr. LeTourneau and were introduced to the brother of the one they came to see. He looked just enough like the one they wanted to warrant a stranger in making a mistake— that is, a stranger working from a photograph. The brother is J. W. LeTourneau. He said, "You want to see Bob. I am Bill. Bob is out in the plant some- where. If you care to walk through the shop with me, we'll probably find him." They eagerly assented, he equipped each with a pair of dark glasses to protect their eyes from the glare of the acetylene torches, and they started out.

The account these two young people gave of their experience that day was later published in *The King's Business*, official Biola publication. It makes stirring reading, even today.

"We followed him into a blast of heat, a glare of sputtering blue flames. Six hooded men bent over a thick piece of steel, all welding at once. The steel is a reversible scraper blade, hot out of the furnace. On our left are the furnaces. On our right we stop to watch an automatic cutting torch—or three work- ing in unison—hissing as they bite three circles simul- taneously out of heavy steel plate. We turn left to watch the battery of saws behind the furnace, singing their way through heavy rounds and bars, slicing off predetermined lengths. Beyond, two carloads of steel are being unloaded. The shop, as far as the eye can reach, is a forest of jib cranes. 'There's Bob,' shouts our guide, and we see a big man, waving his arms, giving his instructions to a group of workmen. He does not see us. He is trying out the first of his new Type U 2-bucket 18-yard Carryalls.

"The try-out is over. We meet R. G. LeTourneau. He takes us through the long shop, past men perched high on upturned scrapers, kindling little blue fires with their electric torches, and at last we stand at the far end of the great plant. Over our heads, across the end of the plant stretches a banner, reading, 'United Crusade for Christ,' in big capital letters, and beneath them in smaller letters, 'Believe on the Lord Jesus Christ and thou shalt be saved.' The sight of that banner gave us a jolt. It is such an extraordinary thing to see in a big industrial plant. What can we say? Here is a man with a vision—one that unmistakably is being honored of God. We find it a bit difficult to say anything. This man definitely chooses to put God first, in life and in business, not because of any material benefit he might reap from the relationship, but because he loves God with his whole heart, and believes He is worthy to be honored and fully trusted.

"He tells us: 'One matter must be kept clearly in mind. The preaching of the Gospel in this plant is not used as a wedge for entrance into the favor of the Almighty. It is not a clever scheme for the increasing of efficiency and the doubling of output. The Gospel is preached solely for the purpose of honoring God and making the employees acquainted with the Lord Jesus Christ. Whatever business successes have ac-

companied this plan—and there have been many—
are merely by-products.'

"We are impressed with his clear thinking, his
energy. He knows what he is talking about!

" 'When hiring a new man, I very seldom ask
whether he is a Christian,' continued Mr. LeTourneau. 'If he can do the work we require, or if he
can learn to do it, he is employed. No record whatever is kept of a man's religious connections. We
have found that twenty-four years of age is the average for our personnel as a whole, first, because every
man must learn a trade, and our methods are different; and, second, because young men have years before them and if won for the Lord Jesus Christ in
their youth, they may spend a lifetime of service for
Him.'

"A whistle blows. 'Come on!' Mr. LeTourneau
says, 'it's meeting time.' He lopes ahead of us down
the shop yelling as he goes, 'Shop meeting, men!'
There is no formal seating arrangement. Many of the
men sit atop of the big machines, on bins, or stand.
Mr. LeTourneau introduces the speaker of the day.
Up steps 'The King's Messengers' quartet, four gradu-
ates of Biola who visited Peoria one day to fill a singing engagement in the town, and when Mr. LeTourneau heard them, he found jobs for them in the shop
so that he could have them handy for singing. They
now present a message in song. After several selec-
tions, enthusiastically received, the speaker of the
day, a visiting evangelist, delivers a simple, straight-

UPPER. Welding scene, Peoria plant.
LOWER. Welding crew, Toccoa plant.

UPPER. Tournapull in action on Hansen Dam, near San Fernando, Calif.

CENTER. Tournapull and Pushdozer leveling runways on Des Moines airport.

LOWER. Scraper stripping top soil for industrial project near Brentwood, Calif.

forward Gospel message followed by a clear-cut invitation. Prayer is offered and the quartet sings again. Any who respond to the invitation, and often some do, have the way of salvation made plain to them. The meeting is over. The men scatter in all directions and resume their tasks. Welding torches resume their sputtering; blue flames begin to blaze; machines start drumming, humming, thumping; lathes and drills and presses are whirring; the hook-tender's whistle shrills for a clear path for seven or eight tons of scraper high in air. The factory is itself again—pandemonium without demons, uproar and disorder controlled and directed by a purpose.

"We wanted to meet the members of the quartet —we were from Biola too. 'These boys,' said Mr. LeTourneau, when he introduced them to us, 'have a burning desire to win souls for Christ. They *live* their Christianity and the men in the shop know it. Their assistance is invaluable in dealing with those who raise their hands for prayer. They often travel with me when I am asked to speak in churches and conferences and their singing is a great attraction. All have work in the plant, suited to their abilities.'

"One of these men was the leader of the shopmen's chorus, about forty in number, all men employed in the plant, which received many invitations to sing in Peoria churches and elsewhere. Their leader told us, 'For the last six months I have been foreman of a department. I began to pray that every one of the twelve men in my department would come to know my Saviour. I am happy to tell you that all but one have taken that step and are rejoicing in the Lord. A Christian, working in an industrial plant, rubbing shoulders with unsaved men, has greater opportunities for soul winning than a mere visitor would ever have.' "

The visit to the Peoria factory which was described so graphically by the two Biola students, from the printed record of which quotations have been taken, was made during the summer of 1936. A visitor to the Peoria factory today, five years later, will find everything as it was then only "bigger and better"—meaning more effectively administered.

Still more interesting is a visit to the Toccoa factory. The Toccoa plant is now as large as the Peoria plant. Besides the factory, there are the farm and the conference grounds—not to mention Toccoa Falls Institute a few miles away. All of which multiplies and intensifies the visitor's interest.

Recently a newspaper announcement stated that the big Toccoa factory of R. G. LeTourneau, Inc., had accepted a contract from the Government to make one million steel shell forgings. How does Mr. LeTourneau, asked a newspaper man, reconcile serving God and producing war materials? The reporter asked the question and received the following answer:

"Scripture clearly teaches Christians," said Mr. LeTourneau, "to be loyal to the powers that be—to their Government. There is a place for meekness, but that doesn't mean that to be a Christian a man has to be a coward.

"The pacifist position doesn't hold water. If a robber came into your house and started abusing your wife and children, you'd fight. It's just a question of whether you want to wait until he gets into your house, or meet him at the front gate.

"We did not seek this work. It is for defense, not aggression. And don't ever forget—the aggressor nations would stamp out Christianity if they ever got control."

Early in his industrial career R. G. LeTourneau became convinced that welding, as a manufacturing process, would revolutionize manufacturing in many lines. He applied himself to a study of its possibilities with characteristic energy and thoroughness. To-day he is widely quoted as an authority on welding. In the present world emergency, he sees welding as a powerful ally in speeding up national defense. Never was time more valuable. To show how welding saves by simplifying design and engineering, by eliminating pattern drawings and pattern making, and by reducing machining time, Mr. LeTourneau recently gave an industrial publication called *Timely Ideas* a detailed technical description, and permitted them to make photographs of important operations, of the building of a seven-hundred-ton press which his company turned out in thirty-five working days.

The first photograph showed Mr. LeTourneau in the cabin of his airplane, 7000 feet up, sketching the first designs. This was on July 2. By July 15 the engineering department had drawn complete plans and the standard structural shapes were cut and ready for fabrication. On August 21, just thirty-five working days from the sketching of the first designs, the press was finished.

Two days before this press was completed, on August 19, a great personal tragedy occurred in Mr. LeTourneau's family. His oldest son, Donald, for whom he had a great affection, lost his life in an airplane crash near Canton, North Carolina, while he and a companion were traveling to Morristown, Tennessee, to deliver some machinery parts.

The sudden death of these young men was a great shock to their many friends and to their families. To Mr. and Mrs. LeTourneau, whose plans were so completely centered about a future with Donald taking a prominent part in all their business and Christian interests, this tragedy was a staggering blow. When the sad message was brought to Mr. LeTourneau, he was stricken with such grief as only one of a nature deep as his could feel. Friends who came and put their arms about him, while burning tears coursed down his cheeks, could find no words to allay the first passionate outbreak of that grief. Human comfort avails nothing at such times. That he was not long in finding the only source of true comfort was soon apparent to those about him. Six days after the accident he filled an annual speaking engagement at the Winona Lake Bible Conference, addressing an audience of several thousand people gathered in the Billy Sunday Tabernacle.

From the time Mr. LeTourneau made the original sketches for the 700-ton press, which was completed two days after the death of Donald LeTourneau, he had given Donald full charge of engineering and construction of the press. Therefore, the successful execution of the task, in record-breaking time, stands as a memorial to the son.

Less than three months before his death, Donald married Miss Wilma Morris, of Hartwell, Georgia, a student with Donald at Toccoa Falls Institute. The young widow, a born-again Christian believer, sent this message to all who wrote to her in her sorrow: "The Lord has wonderfully sustained us all with the consciousness of His abiding presence and the knowledge that one day we too shall be like Him when we see Him face to face."

The portrait here presented of R. G. LeTourneau would not be complete without the mention, just made, of the effects of Donald's death upon him. We get to know a person by seeing him in various situations, at different stages in his development, and by talking with friends about him, and sometimes by talking with his enemies. But true Christian believers have no enemies in the worldly sense. There are worldly people who count them queer if they are unsuccessful in a financial way, or "crazy like a fox" if they are successful in a financial way, by which they mean there's method in their madness. But saneness, discernment, and soundness of judgment, characterize R. G. LeTourneau. His attitude toward life is friendly—openly so. He has a happy disposition, buoyant optimism, and a lively sense of humor. He enjoys his home, his work, his friends, and, above all, his Christian privileges of presenting the Gospel of the Lord Jesus Christ to everyone who will listen to him. He has a contagious laugh and punctuates his public addresses with chuckles—in the right places. He once said, "My principal planks in life are Speed, the Welding Torch, and the Bible." He likes to say that he came up from bankruptcy four times, first, moral bankruptcy, when he was saved; second, spiritual bankruptcy, when he became God's business man; third, financial bankruptcy, when he gave the Lord the first fruits of his financial increase; and fourth, physical bankruptcy, when the Lord restored him to health after the automobile accident in which five others lost their lives. Today he stands, he says, "a living witness that the Lord Jesus Christ, who intercedes for me at the right hand of God, is sufficient for body, soul, and spirit; and finances, too!" Whatever he has to say on the subject of the faith that is in him, he says with irresistible conviction.

One thing more: He's a man's man—big and husky, hale and hearty. He has the bluffness of the outdoors and the roughness of the shop about him. Coat off, sleeves rolled up, hat pushed back, he thoroughly enjoys his physical tasks. He likes to get around and know people. Maybe that's one reason—among many others—why they wanted him for international president of the Gideons.

But that's a story of itself.

XV

President of the Gideons

AT THE Forty-first Annual Convention of The
Gideons held at Hollywood, California, July
25, 1940, R. G. LeTourneau was elected International President. He served the organization in that
capacity for one year, and then resigned because of
the pressure of business and other duties.

While the ballots were being counted, Mr. LeTourneau said, "When someone first mentioned my taking this position, my thought was 'No.' Then I said
I would do anything that God wanted me to do. I
would like to see this layman's organization get Christ
in its heart. I believe that the day has come when
God is going to bring a revival through the laymen
and not the ministers. I do not know just how I am
going to do this job. You are going to have to help
me and we will do it."

Every Christian traveling man, and many Christian
business men, know about The Gideons—and many
other people, Christian and non-Christian, know
about them too. In the autumn of 1898 the Holy
Spirit brought two Christian traveling men together
for the first time in a crowded hotel in Boscobel, Wis-

consin. Each discovered the other to be a Christian and they had their evening devotions together. The next time they met was in Beaver Dam, Wisconsin, on May 31, 1899, on which occasion they arranged to meet again a month later in Janesville, Wisconsin. They met in Janesville on July 1, and a third Christian traveling man joined them. The three formed an organization for "mutual recognition on the road and the winning of other traveling men for Christ." They knelt in prayer and asked the Lord to give them a suitable name for their organization. One of the men arose, read Judges 6 and 7, and said, "We will be called 'The Gideons.' "

From 1899 to 1908 five men served The Gideons as president, and nine annual conventions were held. At the 1908 convention the distribution of Bibles in hotel guest rooms was started. In the next eighteen years three men served for varying terms as president, and 750,000 Bibles were distributed. In 1925, at the annual convention in Columbus, Ohio, during the presidency of Mr. Samuel R. Boggs, head of the Model Mills Company, Rug Manufacturers, Philadelphia, The Gideons became international, and the name was changed to "The Gideons International." A descriptive subtitle reads, "The Christian Commercial Men's Association of America." An office is maintained at 202 South State Street, Chicago. International presidents following Mr. Boggs, now deceased, have been Mr. Samuel A. Fulton, President of The Fulton Company, West Allis, Wisconsin; Mr.

Paul A. Westburg, Western Manager of the Western Electrical Instrument Company, Chicago; and Mr. W. L. Hardin, Building Contractor, Atlanta, Georgia. Mr. Hardin was succeeded in 1940 by Mr. LeTourneau.

At the present time The Gideons have a membership of about five thousand regular members and an equal number of associate and contributing members. The purpose of the association is to place Bibles in hotels, hospitals, penal institutions, and public schools. More than 1,800,000 Bibles have been distributed to date, with thousands going out each month as rapidly as funds are procured. Permission has recently been granted The Gideons to distribute Testaments and Psalms to the Armed Forces; a special edition to sell at twenty-five cents each is now in distribution. It is estimated that 1,300,000 copies will be distributed during the first year and about one million each year for the next four years.

As to how he became a member of The Gideons, Mr. LeTourneau has an interesting story which he tells:

"When I lived in Stockton, California, some of the boys who were members of The Gideons used to call on me when they were in town. One regular caller was a man I had known from boyhood—Harry A. West (of Portland, Oregon; now a trustee). Whenever he was in town he'd call me on the telephone and say, 'Bob, you ought to take out a life membership.' I'd say, 'Yes, I guess I will,' but I

never did, and it went on that way from year to year.
Then came a bad year for me, when I didn't know
from one day to the next whether the sheriff was
going to put a lock on the door or not. Just about
that time another brother Gideon came to town—
Sam Fulton (of West Allis, Wisconsin; later international president). He telephoned me, 'Bob,
we've rounded up a few Gideons and want you to
come to the hotel and join us.' I think my membership had been dropped. I hadn't been able to keep it
up. I said, 'All right,' and we had a meeting with
about a dozen others who were interested. We talked
about getting organized in our town. Then God
spoke to my heart—'How about that life membership
you said you were going to take out and didn't?' I
said, 'Yes, Lord, but this year is the worst year of
all.' Again I heard the still small Voice, 'You know
why you are in this condition.' I said, 'All right,
Lord, I don't know how I am going to get by, but I'll
dig up the money somehow.' Well, friends, I dug it
up and I never missed it."

That's the story in his own words as to how and
when R. G. LeTourneau ceased being an in-and-outer
as a member of The Gideons and became a life member. Many distinguished business men, distinguished
both for their business ability and their Christian vir-
tues, have served as president of The Gideons. No
former president ever qualified on both counts more
fully than R. G. LeTourneau when he was elected
International President at the Forty-first Annual Con-

vention. Upon this occasion he made an address to which he gave the title, "Let's Have a Sixth Column," which had as its theme text the singularly appropriate words, because of the Association's great central purpose, of Hebrews 4:12. Part of the address follows:

"Is not the hour overdue for the mobilization of the Christian forces of the world? Should not the battalions of believers marshall their forces to lead the nations back to God? Should not our sword be the Word of God—the Bible—which has a double edge?—'The Word of God is quick, and powerful, and sharper than any two-edged sword!'

"Just as God called the men of old to do certain things, I believe He is today making that call more especially to commercial men to witness that the Gospel is still the power of God unto salvation. We commercial men have no conflict with the preachers who are preaching salvation through the blood of Christ. But when we laymen who rub shoulders with people in the world every day tell them that Jesus Christ is the solution to all our problems, they sit up and take notice, for they can't say of us as they sometimes say of the preachers, 'They get paid for it.'

"When we sell machinery, we have to demonstrate to the contractors that it will do the job. So in order to get the Gospel over to this unbelieving world, we laymen are going to have to be demonstrators, both by our lives and with our lips. The people of the world think the Gospel is only a theory like other religions; it is up to us laymen to show them that it is practical. Many of us are proving daily that Christianity and business will mix. That God is daily calling more and more business men to witness to the power of the Gospel is one of the most encouraging signs of the times.

"The first thing we must give out is the Bible. It is the backbone of our civilization. As Gideons we first organized for Christian fellowship. Then we had a broader vision, to put the Bible in every hotel room throughout the land. Later came another vision, to put the Bible in the schools, where it is needed most of all. This is our big task today. Let us ask God to help us and go at it in earnest. If each one of us would ask God what He wanted us to do, and if we would do it, we'd get these Bibles into the schools 'in nothing flat.'

"I sometimes wonder if we really grasp what it means to believe in God. One time, when I was in financial difficulty, I sat talking to my banker, who had loaned me a lot of money and was worried. Suddenly he turned to me and said, 'Bob, we believe in you!' I never heard a business man say that to another business man before. But I knew what he meant. Ever since that day, John 3:16—'Whosoever believeth in him'—has meant more to me. This banker was willing to trust me with his money, and I am in business today because he was. If we believe in God, we will trust him.

"I am traveling over the United States and Canada every week-end, and several nights during the week, trying to give out this message. The need of the nations is a Blitzkreig of the Bible."

In his Peoria speech before The Gideons, which has already been referred to, Robert LeTourneau went more fully into what has always been a favorite theme with him when speaking to business men, "Bridging the chasm between the secular and the divine." He delights to point out that Christianity and business *will* mix, if given the chance, and that too many people think they must keep their work and their Christian life as far apart as possible. It is his conviction that God has special work for every one to do right where they happen to be, whether it is as head of a business, working in an office, or out on the road selling—that the layman has opportunities for presenting the Gospel which the preacher does not have.

His speeches are profusely illustrated with his personal experiences. Here are a few examples, taken from his first Gideon address:

"One day I took a man through our plant, gave him a history of the progress we have made, and showed him some of the machines. When we got back to the office, he said, 'This certainly is a testimony of what a man can do.' I said, 'No, brother; you've got it all wrong. It is a testimony of what God can do for a man.'

"When we put the last few additions on to our Peoria factory—a building 160 by 600 feet—we decided that before we put in the machinery, it would be a good place to have a revival—plenty of open

space. Some of you preachers ought to have a tabernacle that size. We put in seats for about 3000 people. I'm not much of a promoter. I'm just a mechanic
whom the Lord has blessed. But I've got some fellows in that factory who know how to promote things,
and all I've got to say is, 'Let's get going!' and they
go. I said, 'Boys, get busy and advertise this thing
and see if you can't get the town in here.'

"We had that place nearly full. When the time
came for the meetings to begin in the evening, we
shut down the other part of the plant and had the
men take seats and listen to the message. There were
several hundred on duty at the time.

"We probably have a thousand men working in
our two factories (Stockton and Peoria). I sometimes say, 'If I could get every one of those men to
come to work with the desire in his heart to see the
firm succeed, regardless of who got the credit for good
work, or who'll get a raise—if they didn't care about
anything else but the firm's success, no competition
could get within forty miles of us.' I say to you tonight that I believe God is looking for a bunch like
that. My Bible says, 'Cast all your burdens on the
Lord.' It's a sin to worry. Folks come to me with
problems, and I listen to them, but sometimes I wonder. One man said to me, 'Brother, I've lost all my
backing. I have nothing back of me but God.' Poor
fellow! Some people claim the Lord has sent them
to me for help. Maybe He has, but He didn't tell
me about it. Perhaps He will. What we need is a

realization of the power, the glory, and the majesty of God.

"A man said to me, 'Brother, I'm going to lose my home if you don't help me.' Now, I want to be tender, reachable, like the Master. I know I'm inclined to be hard and sharp, but I don't mean to be. I want to show the love of God in my own life. But do you know the thought that strikes me when I get a plea like that? I think, 'Who knows but what God might take that home away from him and give him two better ones in place of it?' Do you see what I mean? Are we seeking the kingdom of God? I wonder if it is the home we are seeking instead of God's kingdom.

"Not long after I told the Lord I would try to be His business man and serve Him in that way, I was employed by a big contractor in California. Having turned things over to the Lord, the work seemed to go better. I was trying to secure a large job on which I thought I could make a lot of money, but hadn't got the final decision. I said to myself, 'The Lord can touch that fellow's heart and convince him that I'm the right man to do the work.' So I began to pray, 'Now, Lord, convince that fellow that I'm the right man. He will give me the job. I'll make some money and get this thing going.' It is wonderful how much faith we have when what we want is almost in our hands. I really prayed about that thing. My wife says she likes to hear me tell of this experience because she has never forgotten how down in the dumps

Upper. Logging contractor uses Bulldozer for building truck and skid roads.

Center. Rooter tearing up concrete slabs of old roadbed.

Lower. Angledozer building construction road on All-American Canal in California.

UPPER. R. G. and the 700-ton press, designed and built in 35 working days.

LOWER. R. G. and son Donald in consultation on 700-ton press.

I was when I came home that night and told her I didn't get it.

"I went out with my tractor the next morning wondering what to do. A fellow came along and said, 'I'm pulling up some stumps on my farm. I believe you could pull them cheaper and better with that tractor than I could.' Well, I wasn't much interested. It was a half-day's job. I wanted a big job. I wanted to make a lot of money. I didn't want to fool around with a little job and I turned up my nose at it. But he was insistent. I thought, 'Maybe the pickings will be kind of slim this winter. Better take what I can get.' I put a price on it that was plenty high. He said, 'All right, let's go.' So I moved the tractor up and started pulling out stumps. In spite of the high price I charged him, he was satisfied, because he was still ahead of the game.

"I hadn't finished with him before another farmer came along and said, 'I've got about the same job on my farm. How about coming over?' I said, 'I can't afford going from one farm to another without charging for the time lost.' He said, 'All right.' So I moved over to his farm and did his job. To make a long story short, I kept going like that from one farm to another, with never more than a few days' work at a time, and didn't lose a single hour for four months. And the profit I made was double what I would have made from the job I prayed so hard to get, and lost.

"A lady wrote me a letter saying, 'Brother, I heard your testimony of how you gave your business to the

Lord. I decided it was a good idea, so I did the same thing. Now my business is on the rocks. What am I going to do?' I wrote back to that lady and said, 'Sister, from the tone of your letter I judge you are quite perturbed. If you gave your business to God, what are you worrying about?' I don't mean to be rude, but you see what I mean. Sometimes God has to take the things of earth away from us in order to get our hearts and our affections set on things above.

"I say to folks who are continually crying, 'Oh, if I didn't have to worry about clothes to wear, and food, and shelter—if I could just take a rest!' I say to them, 'Why don't you go to jail?' My idea of heaven is a place where we go to do something. I don't know what God has for me to do. God is trying to train us down here in life for what He wants us to do in heaven. He has lots for you to do if you will say, 'Lord, here I am. Take me and use me and send me out to do Thy will.'

"I want to throw this suggestion out to some of you men who have factories. Preach the Gospel to your people. Don't be afraid. God will see you through."

On January 19, 1941, the largest single distribution of Bibles ever made by The Gideons—twenty thousand Bibles to the schools of Georgia—was dedicated at a special service at the Atlanta Civic Auditorium. Many notables participated in the exercises and Mr. LeTourneau's company built a special display in the form of an immense red cross, 13 feet wide by 18 feet high, composed of the red edges of 1380 Gideon Bibles. The framework of this cross was fabricated of steel in the company's Toccoa plant, and weighed 1200 pounds. Mr. LeTourneau made the principal address. What he said in that address is best summarized in a brief statement which he wrote for the March, 1941, number of *The Gideon* monthly magazine, and printed on the inside front cover of that issue:

"I stood on the platform of the City Auditorium at Atlanta, Georgia, before a fine audience. Behind me was a great wall of Bibles, some of them standing out in relief to form a cross nearly twenty feet high— twenty thousand Bibles being dedicated to the schools of Georgia.

"I spoke of the power of the Gospel, for I have proven that it has not lost its transforming power, and I made a statement that sounded a little fantastic, but the more I think of it, the more sure I am that it is true. I said, 'There's enough power in one page of one of these Bibles to stop Hitler's army if only the truth contained therein could be soaked into hearts.' What a power! Bloodshed and strife, misery and massacre, selfishness and hatred, cannot be stopped by the great engines of mechanical power that man has devised. It takes the power of the Gospel.

"A steam engine converts only six per cent of the heat units in the fuel it uses into actual power. A gasoline engine does better than this. It turns about sixteen per cent of the potential power of the fuel into power. But the Diesel engine can get approximately thirty-three per cent efficiency from its fuel, and that is one reason why the Diesel motor is coming to the front so fast.

"How many of us are steam-engine Christians? One of the great hindrances to mechanical efficiency is friction, and even though we overcome a lot of its effects by the use of oil and other lubricants, it still exists. Friction between groups and individual Christians steals the power from them! Let us ask God to reduce this loss with the 'oil' of His blessed Holy Spirit filling our lives."

XVI

Business Man's Message

TO SAY that a man writes his character in his work, is another way of saying that a tree is known by its fruit. R. G. LeTourneau has built up a business which during 1940 totaled $10,740,845.51 in sales. The visible evidence of his work as an industrialist is represented by three factories at Stockton, California; Peoria, Illinois; Toccoa, Georgia and Sydney, Australia; by nearly 3000 employees; by the manufactured products made by these employees and three factories, which are to be found throughout this country and various parts of the world. Or, because the visible things do not always reveal the uses to which they are put, it can be said that Mr. LeTourneau's work is to be found in our highways, dams, playgrounds, reservoirs, and in many other public works where land-leveling machines facilitate the moving of dirt quickly in vast quantities. He plays an important part in the industrial panorama of these present days.

Human nature is perverse. In one breath people say, "It's not so much what a man *is* that counts, as what he *does*," and in the next, "I'd rather be right than President." Each individual's point of view is apt to be obscured by the amount of money he possesses or does not possess.

R. G. LeTourneau is a successful business man. He is also a successful Christian. These two statements seem like a contradiction. Why? Because a successful business man must sell at a profit if he hopes to keep on selling at a profit. And a Christian is told to "do good, and lend, hoping for nothing again." However, the contradiction is no greater than "what things were gain to me, those I counted loss for Christ." If, therefore, the visible evidences of LeTourneau's work as a business man are the tangible results in buildings, employment, and the general usefulness to society of LeTourneau products, then the visible evidences of his work as a Christian should be something similarly tangible, such as number of souls saved, sick people visited and healed, poor people fed and clothed, the Gospel preached to those who sit in darkness, and a list of gifts to men and causes.

No such inventory could ever be compiled—"Paul planted, Apollos watered, but God gave the increase" —wheat and tares must grow together until the harvest—"not of works, lest any man should boast." Attempts to catalog the results of an evangelist's work, even one whose ministry was as universally acknowledged to be successful as D. L. Moody's or Billy Sunday's, would show nothing conclusive or satisfactory. Any attempt to catalog the results of a Christian lay-

man's ministry would be as repugnant and as mean-
ingless as applause at prayer meeting.

But his witness and testimony! That's different.
What does he say when he walks out there before the
people? This man has a name that he made God his
business partner and because of it the business has
become a business of multimillions, 90 per cent of
the earnings of which have been given away. He is
being invited by church groups and luncheon clubs of
business men to come and tell them about it. Every
week-end finds him at some place far away from his
own direct business interests, giving his simple testimony on God's dealings with him. He speaks as
many as seven times every week-end before as many
different groups, from the time he steps into his airplane on Friday night or Saturday morning until he
returns to business Sunday night or Monday. He
averages three addresses a week between week-ends.
He is dated up for two years.

What does he say? His testimony is intensely personal. He has a simple direct style. He speaks about
practical everyday things out of his own experience.
He has a few familiar texts, which most Christians
committed to memory when they were very young or
when first converted, like Matthew 6:33 and Romans
1:16. Other often-referred-to verses are 2 Corinthians
8:9; Acts 16:31; Job 42:5; and the one after which
the plant publication Now is named, 2 Corinthians
6:2. He talks on the platform as he talks in the shop,
using words anybody can understand. His style is as

clear as crystal, his voice is loud and carries far. A newspaper reporter said of it, "It has the sound of a boulder bounding down a granite mountain."

The quotations which follow are taken from many talks. His illustrations give interesting pictures of incidents in his factory life and show the intimate relationship between his work in the world and his faith in God.

"I want to talk to you about the power of God— Romans 1:16. I like something that's got power. I haven't much use for this half-hearted Christianity. The Gospel that the Apostle Paul is talking about is something real. We each take to our vocations—one man is a preacher and talks about the power of God as a theory, and another man who is a layman talks about the practical side of it. It's all right for the preacher to talk to you about the theory of how it *ought* to work, but it is up to us laymen to tell you how it *does* work. I would like to talk to you about the *power* of the Gospel.

"One reason for that is because I deal with power in machinery. We build a heavy class of machinery. We recently brought out a new machine which is perhaps the most powerful thing that runs on wheels. It has a 165 horse-power Diesel engine. That's the largest that has been built. A machine of 165 horse-power doesn't mean much to the ordinary man, but it is a lot of horses—a lot of power. This machine has pneumatic tires that stand away up above your head.

This machine will open its mouth and pick up eighty-thousand pounds of dirt. When you have a machine that will take a weight like that and move it around at about thirty miles an hour—that's power.

"I like my machines and they work. And the Gospel of Jesus Christ works too. When it comes to speaking about the power of the Gospel, I am like the Christian who had an argument with a man who was not. The man who was not said he was going to beat up the Christian the next time he saw him. The Christian decided that the best way to avoid that was to keep out of the other fellow's way. He did it successfully for a time and then one day he ran right into him on the street. He saw that it was no use trying to escape, so he stepped up to him and said: 'Say, would you mind if I do a little praying before you start in?' The other said, 'You'd better be doing some praying and you'd better be doing it now.' The Christian dropped on his knees and prayed: 'Oh, Lord, help me to give this fellow the worst beating he ever had in his life!' When he opened his eyes and looked up, the man was gone. Later a friend asked the man who ran away, 'What was the matter—you're not yellow, are you?' He replied, 'No, I'm not yellow, but I wasn't going to fight him and God too.' "

"I believe the secret of the power of the Gospel is to be willing to go all the way with the Lord. I believe a man who is on the fence cannot enjoy the things of God. I believe when he tries to get betwixt and between, he gets into an awful mess.

"We had an experience at Boulder Dam that illustrates this point. A group of powder men had been working all night drilling holes in the mountain side to blast away the rock. They wanted to make the big shot before the day crew came on. At last the holes were all dug, the dynamite was in, the wires connected with the power line. The man who was to set off the blast was short of wire and there wasn't time to send to camp for more. What wire he had wasn't long enough to let him get beyond the danger zone of falling rocks. He saw a little cave in the mountainside and thought he'd push the button and jump in there. So he pushed the button, the blast went off, he jumped in the cave—and there was a rattlesnake! He was betwixt and between. He couldn't go in on account of the snake and he couldn't go out on account of the falling rocks. What could he do? He saw a huge rock at the cave entrance. In less time than it takes to tell it, he picked up that rock, dropped it over the snake and jumped into the cave. The snake rattled and rattled but couldn't reach the man because it was pinned down by the rock.

"I wonder sometimes whether some folks who say they are Christians really believe in the Lord or not. I don't know whether they have been born again. They're on the fence. They're betwixt and between. I want to say that you're like that man in the cave and you'll have to do something about it. If you get hold of the rock Christ Jesus, that will save you. He can hold Satan down."

"When temptation gets hold of you young folks, you feel that you just can't resist. That's the power of sin. But the power of God is bigger than the power of sin. When you feel yourself slipping, say, 'Lord help me! God help me!' And something will happen. There will be a victory right then and there. He can change our hearts, He can change our lives, He can change our dispositions, He can change our desires. That's the power of the Gospel. That's what we mean when we say, 'Ye must be born again.'

"I had an experience that shows how simple it is. We were building a dam in the Sierra Nevada Mountains. It was up in a very remote region which was hard to get to. We had three tractors, which had to be driven up under their own power from the railroad siding up a steep and tortuous mountain road to the dam site. Two of these tractors started out and almost made it—scraping and tearing and pulling. But the third didn't seem to have the power. We started the motor and listened. I heard something in that motor. I stopped it. I pulled a pair of pliers out of my hip pocket and set the magneto ahead one turn of the nut. We started the motor again, got into gear, and up that road we went. When we got up to where the other two tractors were, we found they couldn't get any further, while our tractor made it.

"What I want you to understand from this story

is that all it takes to put power in our lives is one touch of God. It isn't a matter of education. The moment you and I say, 'Lord, here am I. Put that power in my life,' that moment God will do that very thing for us."

"God loves us just as I love my children. I have a boy about seventeen. We had a hard time bringing him under control. I used to take him out on construction jobs when he was nine years old. We had a car which we used on these jobs and one day one of the men came to me and told me he had seen this boy driving the car alone. He said, 'I met him on the construction road, and I said to him, "I'll run you a race," but the fellow with me said, " 'Don't say anything to that boy about running *him* a race because he'll run *you* a race." ' That's how much he needed to be kept under control.

"It wasn't long before he wanted his own automobile so he could go places. He probably thought to himself many a time, 'I wonder why my dad can't afford to give me a big high-powered automobile with plenty of gas in the tank and let me rush around and have a good time.' But I haven't seen fit to do it. I might have ruined him if I had. But when he will come to me and say, 'Dad, I'd like to have the car tomorrow. I want to bring a lot of my buddies to church and Sunday school,' why I'll let him have the car and don't you forget it. When he takes that attitude he'll find that nothing is too good for him. Folks, when we take that attitude toward the Lord, we'll find there's nothing too good for us."

"I may not know too much about theology—maybe my grammar ain't very good—but I am glad I know a little about the power of the Gospel. I was over to Niagara not long ago and they told me as I viewed those Falls, 'You haven't got an eye for beauty,' because I got my pencil out and figured how much power was going to waste. How much power there would be in an audience like this if we harnessed just a little of the power of God that's available for each one of us. I saw a tractor working on a big construction job. The operator on the tractor wasn't very much experienced, and as he left the excavation pit the scraper that was hooked behind the tractor broke loose and he didn't know it and rode up to the fill with nothing to fill, and it looked silly—that big powerful tractor with nothing hooked up to it. I wonder if the trouble with a lot of us isn't that we are unhitched from God and don't know it."

"I want to talk to you about some of the things that the Lord has done for me, not as a preacher, but as a business man. A colored man said to his pastor, 'I done got saved last night.' The pastor said, 'That's fine. You gonna quit your sinnin'?' He said, 'I'se done quit already.' 'Fine,' said the pastor. 'You gonna pay up your debts?' 'Now wait a minute, parson,' said the colored man. 'You're not talkin' religion now. You're talkin' business.'

"Some people say that religion and business won't mix. Well, they used to say that oil and water won't mix either, but in our manufacturing plants where we operate a lot of machine tools we use thousands of gallons of oil and water for cooling the tools as they run at high speed. It is a white mixture that looks like milk, but actually it is oil and water with a third ingredient added that causes the oil and water to mix. Religion and business will mix when the Lord Jesus Christ enters the human heart."

"Some people say you can't be a Christian and stay in business. I say I couldn't stay in business if I wasn't a Christian. Some of you may have seen my annual report to the stockholders of our company. A friend said to me, 'Didn't it take a lot of courage to write that report?' I said, 'No, it doesn't take any courage if you believe it.' I said some things in that report about flying to all parts of the country to give the Gospel to many different denominations and creeds, to churches, to schools, to radio audiences. We preach the Gospel also to our people in the factory because we believe that Christianity makes men better mechanics, better accountants, and better superintendents.

"We in America have enjoyed the highest standard of living of any country on this globe. I firmly believe it is because our forefathers came here seeking freedom to worship God, and God has blessed our land. But I wonder if we haven't been getting away from the God of our forefathers. I wonder if we haven't been worshiping the almighty dollar more than Almighty God, Who made this world and all the dollars that are in it. I wonder if what this country needs isn't to go back to the God of our forefathers and seek Him first.

"Go to any industrialist and ask him and he will tell you that there is enough raw material in our land from which to provide plenty for every one, and it doesn't take anything but labor to produce it. We could have the finest of food on our tables. We could all have the finest automobiles and electric refrigerators, air-conditioned steel homes, radios, and the best of clothes—even the poorest of us—if we would follow the principles that our Lord Jesus Christ laid down. If we would seek first the kingdom of God and His righteousness, He would add all of these things."

"Some people think we are doing God a favor by doing right, but we are really doing ourselves a favor. Sin carries its own punishment. In these days, when Communism is sweeping the land, one does not know what the young people will have to face. Communism is the doctrine of hatred; Christianity is the doctrine of love.

"I was brought up in a Christian home and knew the theory of salvation. I could quote chapter after chapter of the Bible by heart. But I did not want to talk about God. After I was saved I wanted to talk about Jesus and how wonderful it is to be saved.

"God is not like a policeman trying to punish us for what we have done. I had an experience which made a lot of things clear to me. Several years ago, when my children were small, my wife had to go away one evening and left me alone with the children. A maid came in to prepare supper and either my wife hadn't told this maid, or had told her and the maid had forgotten, but there at my place was a dish of raw tomatoes. Now, all the children knew I didn't like them and never ate them and consequently they were never offered to me at meal time.

"The difficulty was that we had been doing some disciplining of the children. They would say they didn't like certain things. I don't believe in being too tough about it, but I insisted that at least they ought to taste them before refusing to eat them. Well, here we were, and there were the raw tomatoes at my place, and the children knew I didn't like them, and they were all watching me. I was in a bad fix. I had to do something and do it quickly. Do you know what I did? I picked up my knife and fork and started eating those tomatoes, smacking my lips as if I really liked them. The children didn't know what to think. Not a word was said. Do you know that from that day I like raw tomatoes—especially if you'll put a little mayonnaise on them?"

"We're living in a day when there seems to be so

UPPER. Mr. and Mrs. Donald Philip LeTourneau, married on the
day of Donald's graduation from Toccoa Falls Institute, May 28,
1940.
LOWER. Father and son, a few days before the fatal accident.

UPPER. Dedication of Don LeTourneau Memorial Hall, Labor Day, 1941, Canandaigua Lake camp; speakers and guests.

LOWER LEFT. The LeTourneau family in front row of procession.

LOWER RIGHT. The bronze memorial tablet.

much of the spirit of hatred and strife in the very atmosphere that I sometimes wonder what we're coming to. They are even teaching it in some of our colleges. Not long ago I was speaking in a little country church. A home-town boy had just come home from college and was saying a few words to the audience before I spoke. He said, 'People are worried about Communism in America. We don't need to worry about that. What we need in America is higher taxes and a redistribution of wealth.' Did I smell something? Yes, sir! Nobody believes in a redistribution of wealth and the putting of men on an equal footing with each other more than I do. I wasn't born with a silver spoon in my mouth. I had the least education of the eight children in our family. I am not so far away from the pick and shovel myself. A man who introduced me to an audience the other day said, 'This man is not allowing his wealth to accumulate and spoiling his family with it.' Somebody may say to me, 'How about that $50,000 Lockheed airplane you have?' In answer to that, I'll say this: I'll give that plane to anybody who will do the job with it that I am trying to do. One man suggested I stay home and let him make the next trip. Then he found out I had three speaking engagements to fill and he backed out. I am like the lady that got on the street car with twelve kids and the conductor said to her, 'Are they all yours or a picnic?' She said, 'They're all mine and it's no picnic.'

"I said they are teaching it in our colleges. They

don't call it Communism but that's what it is. I was reading a speech by the president of a college who said that machinery was to blame for our difficulties. He said, 'When they built the pyramids of Gizeh two thousand years before Christ, we are told it took ten thousand men thirty years to build one pyramid. Today, engineers tell us, one hundred men could build it in a year with modern steam derricks. Look at all the men that puts out of work.' Think of the president of a college making such a statement. I can show it to you in black and white. If all we want to do is to put men to work, why don't we build two or three hundred of these pyramids? I don't know what anybody would want a pyramid for. Airports would be more useful.

"What is wealth? It is nothing but the product of labor. I made this statement down South the other night and a newspaper man took me to task for it. He said, 'But we haven't got the wealth down here; you've got it up North.' I decided to have a little argument with him. I said, 'You've got all the raw material that your heart can wish right here in the South. You've got plenty of men out of work that know how to convert that raw material into different products—buildings, machinery, automobiles. Right over here at Birmingham the Lord put the iron, the limestone, and the coal, the three ingredients of steel, all in the same mountain. All they had to do was roll the raw materials out of the mountain into the furnace and you have your own steel right here in your own Southland. Why then can't you have your finished products?' He said, 'But we had to get Northern capital to build those steel mills.' I said, 'You don't have to do anything of the kind. I have been through those mills. I am familiar with their construction. Those mills are made out of the very iron taken out of that mountain and all you had to do was put men to work to build the mills and then put more of your unemployed men to work to raise crops to feed them.'

"There is something wrong, but it isn't the Lord's fault. We are digging an insulating material out of the ground not more than fifty miles north of our Toccoa factory in Georgia to insulate the steel houses we're building there. For the houses we built at Peoria we used a good many tons of that spun glass they call rock wool, a manufactured product. But the insulating material we found in Georgia is a better product and easier to handle and all you have to do is dig it out of the ground. If the Lord had put it in the ground all ready for our use without our having to do some work on it, that is, in its light and expanded form, it would have been very expensive to transport to the factory. But He put it in the ground in the form of a solid rock, which is small of bulk and inexpensive to transport, so that when we get it to the place where we want to use it, all we have to do is run it through a furnace and it pops like popcorn and expands to ten times its normal volume.

"If there's anything wrong it isn't the Lord's fault. My mother used to tell the story of a man who was too lazy to eat. So his neighbors decided they might just as well bury him alive, and the man was too lazy to offer any resistance. On the way to the graveyard they met a man who wanted to know what was up. They told him the man was too lazy to eat. He said, 'I've got a bushel of corn I'll donate.' The lazy man raised his head and said, 'Is it shelled?' "

"I am going to tell you of a little experience that is very close to my heart, but it carries a truth that I want to get over to you tonight. I have a brother who is just a little older than I am. He had a son. This boy worked for us on construction jobs from his earliest years. He was bright, and very clever around machinery. He was congenial and likable and everybody thought the world of him and would do anything for him. He was able to run a big Diesel engine when hardly old enough to raise the lever. When we quit construction work and went into manufacturing, this boy became a service man for the company. He went around fixing trouble on construction jobs and was doing a wonderful job for us.

"There was an operation going on in the logging country. They had one of our machines. Something went wrong with it and they sent for this boy, who was then twenty-two years old. He started out and drove to within a mile or two of the job, when the road became impassable. A team and wagon were there to meet him and take him the rest of the way. They unloaded the equipment from the car and put

UPPER. R. G. LeTourneau, as International President of The Gideons, participates in Bible dedication.
LOWER. Addressing annual missionary service in The Gospel Tabernacle, New York, October 12, 1941.

"NOT HOW MUCH OF MY MONEY DO I GIVE TO GOD, BUT HOW MUCH OF GOD'S MONEY DO I KEEP FOR MYSELF."

UPPER. Motto.
LOWER. A rare view—R. G. at his desk, dictating.

it on the wagon. Just as they were ready to start, he said, 'I'll cut across the bottom of this hill and meet you on the other side at the turn of the road.'

"He had a gun, and thinking he might run across a rabbit or a squirrel, he took it with him. He had been born and raised in that country and knew it like a book. They saw him start out.

"That was over five years ago and not a sign of that young man has ever been found. The locality has been scoured by scores and scores of people. Large rewards have been posted for information and evidence of what happened to him. He had nothing to run away from as far as we know. We found out sometime afterward that there was a certain thing which happened the night before that he probably saw. If he saw it, it may have broken his heart. In that case, he had a broken heart that morning. But what did he do to himself? If he had done away with himself, there would surely have been evidence left. There were no lakes in the vicinity, or nothing else that he could have fallen into. Every clue was run down. We don't know whether he is alive or dead. I think he is alive. My brother has waited day in and day out, year in and year out. His hair is turning gray, waiting in hopes that some day his son will show up.

"Where is he tonight? Only God knows. I have often thought that sometime I am going to meet him at one of these services. I sometimes think I might see him in the audience and I'll run down and grab him by the shoulders, and take him to the nearest telephone, and call up his father and say, 'I have found him! Here he is!'

"He knows we love him. Why should he stay away? I can't explain it. Neither can I explain why it is that when the God who made you gives you the opportunity, you don't go to Him and give Him the chance to prove His love for you and let Him put the power of the Gospel into your life.

"That's what He is saying to you tonight, and yet you don't come. Oh, I beg of you, don't put it off until it is too late. Will you say to the Lord, 'Lord, what do You want me to do?' And will you do what He tells you to do? God bless you."

XVII

Gospel Headquarters

THE STORY of R. G. LeTourneau would not be complete without a concluding chapter on the work of the LeTourneau Evangelistic Center, located at 1270 Sixth Avenue, New York City.

There at the heart of Rockefeller Center—famous all over the world as "Radio City"—which is itself the heart of the world's greatest city in many fields of human endeavor, including that of Christian evangelization and missionary enterprise, is the control room, so to speak, and the directing center of Mr. LeTourneau's many Christian interests and activities.

The demand for his presence and the inspiration of his testimony as a speaker before all kinds of Christian gatherings brought invitations in increasing numbers from churches, young peoples' societies, Bible conferences, and missionary rallies in widely scattered places. The number of these invitations outran Mr. LeTourneau's available time for the giving of such talks. Without any intention on his part of making a business of public speaking on a national scale, he shortly found himself faced with so many invitations as to leave no time, had he accepted even a small number of them, for managing his business, which was growing in size and complexity at an embarrassing rate of speed.

The story of how Mr. LeTourneau became a speaker is told in Chapter 11, "Personal Evangelism." He began by giving his personal testimony at the meetings conducted by the young people connected with the church he belonged to in Stockton, California, when they took over the services at one of the downtown missions about once a month. A few years later, when the LeTourneau business built its Peoria factory and the Peoria Association of Commerce held its annual banquet, Mr. LeTourneau was invited to attend. After the principal speaker of the evening had made his address, Mr. LeTourneau was asked to tell the company assembled for the banquet how he had chosen Peoria as the location for his factory. This opportunity appealed to him as an excellent one for giving the influential citizens of Peoria his witness as to God's leading in his business affairs, and he took full advantage of it.

What he said on this occasion made such an impression that, following the meeting, he received several invitations to speak in Peoria churches. Before long he found himself spending his week-ends filling these speaking engagements. Other churches and groups heard of his testimony and calls began to come in from audiences and institutions outside of Peoria. Convinced that the Lord was leading him into new fields of Christian evangelization, Mr. LeTourneau made this speaking ministry the subject of earnest prayer, and rejoiced to find the Lord opening new doors. Instead of turning his business over to others to manage, he has chosen, under God, to remain the head of the LeTourneau business and spend the time which other business executives generally give to recreation to preaching the Gospel of the Son of God.

He fills, on the average, seven speaking engagements over a week-end. Once in a while, necessity compels him to interrupt his working schedule with a midweek flight to some far-away city. These midweek calls now average three a week. The need for centralizing his Christian activities in order to avoid wastefulness of time and money, and the desirability of conserving his health and strength, were brought home to Mr. LeTourneau not long after that memorable automobile accident of June, 1937, in which he and Mrs. LeTourneau, and two others, were seriously injured, and in which five persons were killed. Two considerations led Mr. LeTourneau to seek a better mode of transportation than the automobile for his gospel journeyings—the necessity of filling a larger number of speaking engagements by making better time in traveling and the ability to reach far-away places in the week-end and midweek periods.

First, one airplane was purchased, a Waco, cabin-type, five-place, 350 horse power, speed 150 miles per hour. Other airplanes now include a Lockheed 12, Executive Model, seven-passenger, twin motors, 450 horse power, speed 190 miles per hour, range 1200 miles; a three-place cub plane, 80 horse power; and a two-place cub plane, 40 horse power. The last two planes are used for short flights where airports are too small for the larger planes to land.

The necessity referred to of keeping a long list of speaking appointments which must be made a long time ahead, of avoiding duplication, that is, finding himself committed to speak in two or more widely separated cities on the same day, or returning to a city to speak to a group after having spoken in that city a short time previously before a different group; of making sure that those who invite Mr. LeTourneau to visit them do not forget the time of his visit, which is apt to happen when the date is promised a long time ahead—these and other considerations brought it home to Mr. LeTourneau that an operating center, so to speak, was needed at which could be centralized and co-ordinated the handling of his personal appearances before Christian audiences in various parts of the country and where the many other interests and activities connected with The LeTourneau Foundation could be supervised and directed.

Associated with Mr. LeTourneau at the LeTourneau Evangelistic Center, in Rockefeller Center, New York, is a man who for twelve years has been the head and front of a work known to a constantly growing circle of Christian people as the "Interstate Evangelistic Association." This man is Dr. Harold Strathearn, Executive Secretary of this Association. The story of how Dr. Strathearn and Mr. LeTourneau were brought together in the Providence of God is the record of a significant episode in the present history and is of much interest:

During the summer of 1938, when Mr. LeTourneau's mind was taken up more or less with the building of a new factory at Toccoa, Georgia, he happened to be one day in the city of Buffalo, New York. There he discussed with Dr. J. Palmer Muntz, pastor of the Cazenovia Park Baptist Church, of that city, a friend, various matters of general interest to them both, and one of particular interest to Mr. LeTourneau, namely, the management of his speaking activities, which just at that time were a considerable problem to him. Dr. Muntz, who had been associated with Dr. Strathearn for many years in the work of the Interstate Evangelistic Association, suggested that he, Mr. LeTourneau, get in touch with Dr. Strathearn and discuss the matter with him. He was sure, he told him, that Dr. Strathearn was in a position to help in the solution of the problem.

Not long after, on a week-end in November, 1938, Mr. LeTourneau and Dr. Strathearn met in Cleveland, Ohio, at the Christian and Missionary Alliance Church, where Mr. LeTourneau was filling one of his speaking engagements and giving his Christian testimony. The two men talked together for not more than fifteen minutes. So completely did they mutually comprehend what each could do for the other, that with no other basis of agreement or any subsequent exchange of correspondence that could be called a contract, they entered into a relationship which is nothing other than a bond of Christian fellowship and faith. It is worthy of note that no business arrangement, strictly speaking, was ever entered into between them, and none exists to this day. For several years Dr. Strathearn and his organization, the Interstate Evangelistic Association, has directed the affairs of the LeTourneau Evangelistic Center.

The work of the Interstate Evangelistic Association, founded in 1929 in Rochester, New York, by Dr. Strathearn, has gone steadily forward under his leadership. For years the Association's offices have been located in Rochester, at 1403 Temple Building. In March, 1940, these offices were moved to 1270 Sixth Avenue, New York City, and united with those of the LeTourneau Evangelistic Center.

The Interstate Evangelistic Association was started by Dr. Strathearn to fill Baptist pulpits with sound, Bible-believing Baptist preachers, and to check the spread of Modernism in Baptist churches. This unique ministry has been singularly honored of God and during the past twelve years 675 ministers and churches in fifteen States have been helped. The Association gives away over one hundred thousand tracts yearly and maintains a large "Book Room" in which only sound, Fundamental Christian literature is handled.

Another work of the Interstate Evangelistic Association which has grown to large proportions and wide effectiveness under Dr. Strathearn's direction is

Missing nephew, Harlan LeTourneau, son of J. W. LeTourneau,
President of Ace Motors, Inc., Indianapolis, Ind.
UPPER, as he looked when last seen; LOWER LEFT, when married;
LOWER RIGHT, as a boy.

Quick changes of mood characteristic of Board of Directors' meetings, R. G. LeTourneau, Inc. At EXTREME RIGHT, Mr. and Mrs. LeTourneau.

that of the LeTourneau Christian Camp, which was established seven years ago at Canandaigua Lake, Canandaigua, New York, under the name of "The Tabernacle on the Lake," and which was named after Mr. LeTourneau as an expression of appreciation for his generosity to the camp.

The camp has become one of the most popular in the country. Each summer large groups of Christian young people spend their vacations there, combining Bible study and healthful recreation, under consecrated supervision and direction. During the summer of 1941 approximately twenty-four hundred young people spent a week at the camp, and over four hundred boys and girls professed acceptance of Jesus Christ as Lord and Saviour. Scores of others reconsecrated their lives to God's service, and many have announced their determination of entering Bible schools and seminaries for preparation for full time Christian work.

The Board of Trustees of the Interstate Evangelistic Association consists of Rev. Howard C. Fulton, D.D., Chairman; Rev. John Muntz, Bayonne, New Jersey; Rev. Arthur F. Williams, New York, New York; Dr. J. Palmer Muntz, Buffalo, New York; Mr. Matthew Weimar, Orchard Park, New York; and Dr. Strathearn.

The LeTourneau Evangelistic Center was organized in September, 1939, for the purpose of bringing all the evangelistic interests of R. G. LeTourneau under one head. Mr. LeTourneau is President; Dr.

Strathearn, Director; Rev. R. W. Neighbour, Associate Director; and George R. Ives, of Binghamton, N. Y., Treasurer.

The LeTourneau Foundation, under which the LeTourneau Evangelistic Center operates, has been endowed by Mr. LeTourneau for $13,000,000. Besides the interests already named in the present history, Mr. LeTourneau is actively interested in The Gideons, serving as International President for 1940-1941; he is President of The Evangelical Clubs; President of the Winona Lake Christian Assembly, Inc., where the 47th annual session was held during the summer of 1941; and heads, with Mrs. LeTourneau, the work of the Lake Louise Bible Conference Grounds, Toccoa, Georgia.

Through the LeTourneau Evangelistic Center approximately 25,000,000 tracts and pamphlets were given away last year to churches and individuals. From ten to twelve evangelists are regularly employed by the Center to serve churches located in fields unable to support missionaries of their own. As a result of the labor of these evangelists, more than half a million people have heard the Gospel; over 4600 have found Christ as their Saviour, over 6900 Christians have been awakened and have consecrated their lives to God, and 374 who had drifted away from God have been restored to Christian fellowship.

Other activities carried on by the Center are the distribution of fifty thousand Scripture Calendars yearly direct to homes; the publication of an Evan-

gelistic Song Book, edited by Arthur W. McKee, of
Winona Lake, Indiana, nationally known song leader;
the sponsoring of evangelistic programs over the radio
in strategic spots throughout the country; the promo-
tion of children's Bible Clubs in the Northwest section of the United States by one of the ablest children's workers in America, as a result of which
hundreds of children from irreligious homes have
found Christ as their Saviour; and interest in and support of the work of the Intercollegiate Gospel Fellowship in organizing Christian students attending colleges in the New York metropolitan area and helping
them carry on a progressive program of work in presenting Christ to the student bodies of these colleges.

Dr. J. Palmer Muntz, the man through whom,
under God's leading, R. G. LeTourneau and Harold
Strathearn were brought together in their present
association, made the following statement just as this
volume went to press:

"When I suggested to Mr. LeTourneau the ad-
visability of having someone arrange his speaking
itinerary and co-operate with him generally in his
Christian activities, and recommended Dr. Strathearn
as the one most perfectly qualified to render such
service, little did I dream that the LeTourneau
Evangelistic Center with all of its manifold activities
would be one of the splendid results of that association.

"I believe R. G. LeTourneau, because of Dr. Strathearn's intelligent management in the direction of his

speaking appointments, has spoken and is speaking to more people in more churches, large and small, of more denominations, from coast to coast, from Canada to the Gulf, than anyone else has ever been able to do.

"Business men flock to hear him because of what God has done for him in his business. Such men by the thousands have been influenced by his life and testimony, and many of them have been led to a deeper consecration of their time and talents to Jesus Christ.

"I know these things because he has influenced our church as no other man has. He has done me more good than anyone I know. Every time I hear him, he thrills me anew. I have traveled hundreds of miles to hear him speak, and his message has always inspired me with deeper consecration to the cause of Christ.

"Those of us who know Bob LeTourneau best, love him for what he is and not for what he has, and our earnest prayer is that our heavenly Father may keep and guard him, bless and sustain him, and use his life and voice to draw men everywhere to 'follow the Lamb withersoever he goeth.'"